Process-Oriented Healthcare Management Systems

Process-Oriented Healthcare Management Systems

Development, Use, and Maintenance for Patient-Safe Healthcare

Anita Edvinsson B.Cs, CRNA, AOCNS

BEP BUSINESS EXPERT PRESS

Process-Oriented Healthcare Management Systems: Development, Use, and Maintenance for Patient-Safe Healthcare

First published in 2020 by
Business Expert Press, LLC
222 East 46th Street, New York, NY 10017
www.businessexpertpress.com

ISBN-13: 978-1-95152-730-3 (paperback)
ISBN-13: 978-1-95152-731-0 (e-book)

Business Expert Press Health Care Management Collection

Collection ISSN: 2333-8601 (print)
Collection ISSN: 2333-861X (electronic)

Cover and interior design by Exeter Premedia Services Private Ltd., Chennai, India

First edition: 2020

10 9 8 7 6 5 4 3 2 1

Printed in the United States of America.

Abstract

Public opinion polls suggest that most Americans trust their medical team. When people go to the physician or are admitted to the hospital, few of them worry about being harmed by the doctor, or someone else from the medical team making a mistake. Unfortunately, mistakes do happen, and a lot of the adverse events are both preventable and serious. The most common types of preventable harm include hospital-acquired infections, surgical error, wrong site surgery, medication errors, in-hospital injury, misdiagnosis, and deep vein thrombosis. Depending on the set of prevalence data used, preventable harm results in between 210,000 to 400,000 deaths annually in the USA. A far more common outcome than death is serious harm; which affects more than 10 to 20 times more patients than lethal harm. Preventable harm costs billions of dollars every year and inflicts huge suffering for both patients and personnel involved.

Administrators should not be the primary determinant in their ability to deliver safe, effective, and humane care. Many countries struggle with top-heavy systems, in which decisions about how care is provided are made by those who are far from experienced in caring for patients, and who work at the blunt end of the organisation. This must change. Professionals at the sharp end need support, structure and help in organising necessary information to create a safe culture, a learning environment and safe patient care, all at lower costs.

This book shows a new way to health care management by presenting arguments for a new approach together with some concrete advice on how health care executives and practitioners can begin to think and act differently in order to provide safe health care.

The content provides the reader with practical hints on how a process-oriented management system can be designed from a set of principles aimed at accomplishing a solid structure that is both easy to use and easy to maintain. It also illustrates the importance of the change in the patient safety approach, and the direct dependency between leadership and co-creating a safety culture with personnel at the sharp end.

What is the Book About?

This book is a handbook that provides its readers with tools for designing a structure for a management system, as well as the tools for documenting processes within it, where the starting point is based on current safety research.

Who is the Audience for this Book and Why Would they Buy It?

The book addresses medical professionals who have recently acquired leadership and management responsibilities. It is also useful for project members working on reviewing or building a management system to support patient safety. The book content can also be used as a guideline for politicians, public officials, and executives at all levels, or anyone else who works with patient safety and who needs to renew their knowledge about management systems and process orientation.

This hands-on book presents a step- by -step process on how a management system can be formed, the prerequisites for having a management system that supports daily work, and how it can result in increased patient safety. The book contains many utilitarian tips for work procedures for both process descriptions and for the formation and administration of a management system. The examples come from healthcare, but the methodology described in this book can be used in any business.

Keywords

management system; patient safety; healthcare; process; healthcare management; psychological safety; leadership; learning organization; quality; business process; safety-II; operational improvement

Contents

Foreword

Amy C. Edmondson, Professor of Leadership and Management, Harvard Business School; Author, *The fearless organization: Creating psychological safety in the workplace for learning, innovation, and growth.*

This timely and actionable book is about how to make healthcare organizations work as they should—to provide high-quality safe care to patients. Providing better healthcare, as author Anita Edvinsson explains, is not a matter of developing better therapies and technologies but rather primarily a matter of implementing better management. Transforming healthcare delivery calls for nothing less than rethinking how we manage people and processes of care.

Process-oriented healthcare management systems is *timely* because we're running out of time. Healthcare is broken—and everyone close to the industry knows it. For years, in developed economies, we have been spending more on healthcare and getting less—measured in terms of key health outcomes like life expectancy, obesity, maternal health, and preventable patient harm. This book is *actionable* because it offers practical ideas with the potential to transform organizations. Edvinsson wisely emphasizes the work that happens on the front lines of patient care and discusses ways to reorganize processes to support those doing the invaluable tasks that directly affect the patient.

At the core of the book's contribution is the business process approach. Edvinsson tells us how to analyze and alter work processes so that they better serve patients, caregivers, and healthcare organizations alike. A well-designed management system, she explains, can help us ensure that information needed by the staff closest to the patient is available, where and when it is needed. Safety problems are created at all organizational levels, but they show up at what healthcare researchers call "the sharp end" of care—those deeply vulnerable moments where clinicians interact with patients at the bedside. Edvinsson offers a compassionate perspective that puts the particularly painful source of economic and emotional waste created by what's called "avoidable harm" to patients at the very front of the issues needing our attention.

Ensuring patient safety, in particular, is a challenge that thankfully receives considerable attention in this book. To understand why patient safety remains such an intractable issue, it is important to appreciate the risks created by the peculiar combination of human psychology and the complex, customized activities that comprise healthcare delivery.

Consider the following story, a composite vignette I created from my own field notes taken from observations of caregivers in research conducted in multiple hospitals in the United States.

> A nurse working the night shift in a busy urban hospital makes her evening rounds – reviewing patients' treatment plans, taking temperatures, and administering medications. She notices that the dosage for one of the patient's meds seems high. Fleetingly, she considers calling the doctor to check the order. Just as fleetingly, she recalls the doctor's disparaging comments about her abilities the last time she called him at home with a question. Feeling confident that the dose is more than likely to be correct, she pulls the drug from the supply cabinet and heads for the patient's bed.[1]

In this moment of failing to reach out for help—failing to double-check the dose in the face of her slight uncertainty—the nurse has implicitly discounted the possibility of patient harm. Her reluctance to speak up is not caused by a lack of caring about human life; quite the contrary, she has devoted her entire career to caring for the sick. Instead, in that small moment of hesitation in which an opportunity to speak up presented itself, the nurse's brain has exaggerated the importance of the doctor's scorn and downplayed the possibility of patient harm. In my

---

[1] Adapted from Edmondson, A.C., and K.S. Roloff. 2008. "Overcoming Barriers to Collaboration: Psychological Safety and Learning in Diverse Teams." In Team Effectiveness in Complex Organizations: Cross-Disciplinary Perspectives and Approaches, eds. E. Salas, G.F. Goodwin and C.S. Burke, 179-200. SIOP Frontiers Series. Mahwah, NJ: LEA.

research, I have documented countless such moments of silence where voice was needed—not just in healthcare, but in contexts ranging from manufacturing to space exploration.

How is it that silence can prevail even when a work activity is directly and obviously related to human safety, as it is in healthcare? The answer lies in our psychology. Human beings are finely attuned to risk. When it comes to things like preventing patient harm in hospitals a sensitivity to risk ought to work in our favor. The trouble is, we're attuned primarily to *interpersonal* rather than *technical* risk. It's human nature. We don't want to ruffle feathers. We don't want to bring bad news—instinctively appreciating that messengers get shot, even if we're "just the messenger." We don't want to be thought of as stupid; we don't want to be shamed when we erroneously point out a quality problem.

The simple truth is that, even in the absence of bullies and bad bosses, people tend to assume that questions will be scorned, criticism will be badly received, half-baked ideas will be unwelcome, and requests for help will make them look bad. You could say that we spontaneously overvalue maintaining a sense of comfort, security, and belonging *in the moment*, and spontaneously undervalue the vague, probably-won't-happen-any-way, potential failures that might unfold *later*. Psychologists have a term for it—discounting the future—and it's a natural cognitive bias that makes it easy for us to hold back on speaking up even when human safety is at risk. For this reason, I've devoted considerable research attention to what I call "psychological safety"—defined as a workplace climate in which people *do* feel able to speak up with questions, concerns, ideas, and even mistakes. Building climates of psychological safety is particularly important in healthcare, as Edvinsson recognizes, and any reader interested in learning more about the accumulated research on the benefits of psychological safety for reporting behavior (along with learning, collaboration and even performance) in healthcare and other organizations can find more detail in my recent book, *The fearless organization*.[2] But only by reading *Process-oriented healthcare management systems* carefully will those of you who wish to help lead the transformation of healthcare

---

[2] Edmondson, A.C. 2019. *The Fearless Organization: Creating Psychological Safety for Learning, Innovation and Growth*. New York, NY: Wiley.

be equipped to consider the full set of process changes needed. If you're willing to help this vital transformation unfold, then roll up your sleeves, get ready to take notes, turn the page, and enjoy the learning journey that lies ahead.

Endorsements

This book distinguishes itself from others in that it not only provides a unique set of practical examples on how to develop and implement a management, it also focuses on developing a management system based on how work actually gets done and helping to ensure that more things go well, rather than just focusing on negatives. An excellent, helpful, and innovative overview.

Ron Gantt
Vice President
SCM, Safety Compliance Management, Inc

Edvinsson makes a strong case that the current paradigm many western healthcare organizations are operating under results in pain and suffering for patients and their families, managers and staff, and increased healthcare costs, increased errors and inefficiencies. She walks us through how to create, use and maintain what she calls a "Patient Safe" management system based on best practices, shared knowledge, continuous quality improvement and detailed process mapping and facilitation. The results are cultures of trust and collaboration where multiple disciplines work together, there is a focus on the patient and what is working well, and where leaders "walk their talk".

This book is a comprehensive "how to" manual that includes helpful visuals and practical tips and tools based on the author's experiences as a front-line nurse, leader and manager. A recommended read for healthcare leaders and managers.

Pamela Thompson, BN, MSc
#1 Best selling author, global health and management consultant

The book describes how a process oriented management system, already well established in other safety critical industries, can be used in the healthcare industry to ensure patient safety. The principles of the management system are rooted in Safety 2 and the book gives practical. detailed instructions on how to create such a system, with processes that map out "work as done". The book also explains how healthcare differs from other industries and describes how to implement a safety management system within a healthcare organization. Leadership, culture and learning also have central roles to play in patient-safe care and the author explains how the management system must work with these three elements.

I've seen other people advocate for the use of a safety management system in healthcare, but Edvinsson have taken it much further than that. I've certainly not seen anyone giving such detail on the practical steps to take to create one.

Jonathan Hazan
Chairman at Patient Safety Learning
Chief Executive at Perfect Ward

This book is a guiding light for a whole systems approach to the care pathway of the patient that recommends inclusion of all stakeholders involved in the process and has at it's heart the security and safety of the patient all along the value chain. It describes supporting staff in being the best they can in ensuring the optimum level of patient safety. I highly recommend this book to workers in the field of healthcare, in particular nurses and doctors and education facilities.

Ms. Eilish Mc Keown
MCC Coach (ICF) & former Hospital
Administrator in the Irish Health Service

CHAPTER 1

Introduction—Why This Book

The purpose of writing this book can be summarized in one sentence—saving lives and reducing suffering. Saving lives and reducing suffering are the main driving forces for most people who work in delivering health care. These driving forces have their source in a basic ethical value: to help and not to harm.

I have been working within the healthcare sector since 1985. Over the years, I have been working in various types of hospitals, wards, care settings, ICU (intensive care unit), and primary care. I have a specialist nursing degree in anesthesia and oncology, and I have also worked as a ward manager and an operations manager. Alongside that, I also have experience of being a patient and a relative.

Consequently, I have collaborated with a variety of healthcare professionals such as nurses, doctors, mental health nurses, hospital physicists, physiotherapists, social workers, dieticians, radiotherapists, and many more. We have wholeheartedly devoted our time, knowledge, and engagement to giving highly skilled health care, aimed to cure, relieve pain, and bring comfort to our patients and their families. The many unforgettable meetings with patients and their relatives as well as educational collaborations across the boundaries of the professions used to fill my soul not only with desire and a joy for work, but also with courage and vigor to continue, despite a hard workload and often demanding situations.

In my experience, people who work in healthcare professions put high demands on themselves and experience high expectations from others to act professionally. Those demands come from the patients, colleagues, and authorities, meaning, among other things, that the work should put our patient's needs as a starting point. There should be a good collaboration between involved professionals, and care should be given based on science and professional experience. Less experienced colleagues should have the chance to gradually learn increasingly difficult tasks. The personnel are expected to handle advanced technical equipment flawlessly and make many decisions when time is short. Furthermore, healthcare staff have a statutory duty to keep updated with new knowledge, to work promoting patient safety, and to collaborate in the development of operations while always following applicable legislations. This list can be made much longer.

Working in the healthcare business is complex and takes place in a vast context. The workplace consists of different parts that more or less interact with each other, often at many organizational levels. Health care has become increasingly specialized and the patient's pathway to receiving health care is rarely easy. Moreover, the variation in the work is not predictable. Unexpected events occur all the time, for example, the patient's condition may rapidly deteriorate, and it may be very difficult to instantly understand why. The extent of knowledge needed to deliver safe health care is so vast that it is simply impossible to keep all the parts updated in the human brain.

In every workplace I have been working in, information has been written down and at least partly gathered in binders, containing checklists, PMs, instructions, procedure descriptions, telephone lists, caches, and more. The contents of these bindings have been partially overstated, sometimes out of date and sometimes out of context. Occasionally the staff have been informed that information about new procedures has been provided to only some of the staff or written down on loose notes. Subsequently, the notes were hung on message boards and could have ended up under lunch menus. Therefore, a lot of the working time that should have been devoted to direct patient care has instead been taken up looking for correct information. All this wasted time looking for information could have been spent on valuable patient care.

Along with the computerization and introduction of IT in health care, most of the information has been moved to the companies' own intranets and shared storage disks. But even there it is often difficult to find relevant information. There are an enormous number of documents that are far from updated, reviewed, or relevant. In Region Skåne[1] intranet alone there

---

[1]   One of Sweden's largest county councils/regions providing healthcare to approximately ¼ of Sweden's population

are approximately 7 million documents stored. In addition, the intranets are rarely designed in a user-friendly way. Personnel, who depend on accurate and easy-to-access information in their clinical everyday life, are having difficulties finding information they need. Many times, instead of searching for information on the intranet, a colleague is to be asked a question, or people just do as they once have learned. For example, it can take 15 minutes to find the forms to be filled in and to accompany a deceased patient from an ICU to the morgue (I have witnessed that at one of the largest hospitals in Sweden), because of a changed procedure followed by poor information and an inefficient search engine showing irrelevant options.

The need for information may, for example, include questions about how a new piece of equipment works or what blood tests are included in a particular disease investigation. Another example of information needed may be checklists for an examination or a description of the equipment that should be prepared before a certain procedure, for example, inserting a central line.

Each and every time it is difficult to find such information, or if there is doubt as to whether the content can be trusted, there is a risk of missing out. Not only do a waste of time and a waste of resources occur, but risky situations can also emerge. Knowledge that everyone needs can run the risk of becoming individual property rather than being a shared asset. In a state of stress, due to time constraints, complex contexts and difficulties to access important information have made it easier to make mistakes. Mistakes can have serious consequences for the patients and for health-care personnel. Working in health care involves taking risks. This is a fact that we never can get away from. But it is possible to create conditions for as much as possible to go right. One of those prerequisites when thoroughly designed and maintained is a management system.

A management system is a structure for systematically and organically describing the work that is performed on a daily basis in the workplace. It sounds simple, and basically it is simple, but it requires consistent thinking, a certain logic, and an organization that keeps the management system vivid and practically useful. I dare to say it but there is an enormous amount of money wasted in health care, because of poor patient safety, and there are plenty of poorly functioning management systems.

For decades the authorities have reported thousands of people who have been injured or have died in hospitals due to the so-called avoidable harm. This means injuries that have caused patients "suffering, physical or mental injury or illness and death that could have been avoided if adequate measures had been taken in the patient's contact with the health care."[2] In practice, this means that every 10th hospital bed in Sweden is occupied by a patient who is injured by the health care.[3] These damages cost society a great deal of money.

The suffering of patients and their relatives is not priced in this context. Other social costs, such as extended sick leave, reduced tax incomes, reduced purchasing power, healthcare workers' work-related stress, high staff turnover, difficulties in recruiting, staff on sick leave, and staff time to correct the errors, are usually not included in the statistic calculations. Moreover, data concerning costs and amount of avoidable harm to the patients should be interpreted with caution as there is a great deal of underreporting of the adverse events. The lack of recognition of unsafe conditions or practices is one important reason they are not reported.

Based on my experience, I am convinced that a well-designed management system based on knowledge gained from safety research can greatly help to create order and work out procedures, instructions, and much of the information that the staff closest to the patient (which I call personnel at the sharp end) need daily. Safety is created at all organizational levels but shows up next to the patient and that is also where the mistakes occur.

Knowledge in the context affecting the delicate boundary between success and failure is crucial in order for successful development of patient safety. To succeed in making health care safer, a great deal of courage is needed from everyone involved: politicians, boards, owners, managers, professionals, students, and patients. It is necessary to build a strong safety culture, to invest in conscious and present leadership, and to support the work of the committed staff. These three parts—safety culture, conscious leadership, and committed staff—constitute the real management system.

---

[2]   Swedish Patient Safety Act 2010: p. 569
[3]   National Board of Health and Welfare, Situation Report in the Patient Safety Area 2014.

The written information given in a management system is one of many ways to formulate and visualize what happens at the sharp end, when delivering health care. Understanding this is a way to strengthen patient safety and thereby save lives.

My intention for writing this book is to instill courage in all the wonderful and brave people who devote their professional life to the pursuit of doing good and not harm.

Acknowledgments

A huge warm thank you to everyone who has contributed in making this book about management systems for patient-safe health care possible. The professionals who helped me bring the book to life—Linda Keller and Hazel Clarke, for eloquently simplifying the complicated prose; Bethany Walmsley, Ron Gantt, Susan Burnett, Kristina Iritz Hedberg, Synnöve Ödegård, Monica Carlson, Erik Hollnagel, David Dilts, and Amy Edmondson for their support, valuable comments, and engagement; finally, for the unwavering love and support from my wonderful husband Håkan. My writing process would not have come into fruition without all these lovely people and knowledgeable contributors.

Anita Edvinsson

How to Use This Book

Step by step, this book outlines how a management system can be formed, the prerequisites for having a management system that supports the daily work, and how it can result in increased patient safety. The examples are from health care and care settings.

The book contains many practical tips for work procedures, for both process descriptions, and for formation and administration of a management system and primarily addresses medical professionals who have recently acquired leadership and management responsibilities. It is also useful for anyone involved in reviewing or building a management system or students who, following graduation, are going to work within healthcare or other care settings. The book can also be used as a guideline for politicians, public officials, and executives at all levels who work with patient safety.

The content will provide you with practical hints on how a process-oriented management system can be designed, based on a set of principles aimed at accomplishing a solid structure that is both easy to use and easy to maintain. It also illustrates the importance of the change in the patient safety management approach. Another purpose is to bring about insights into the direct dependency between safety and leadership helping you lead toward cocreating a corporate safety culture driven by managers, together with personnel at the sharp end. The expression "at the sharp end" is often used in safety literature and by safety scientists, for example, professor E. Hollnagel or professor S. Dekker, meaning that frontline personnel working closest to the patient are directly involved in the most difficult or dangerous aspects of the work when, for example, delivering treatment and health care.

As there might be legal or qualitative requirements on hospitals and other healthcare settings to identify and manage processes within the management system, there is a chapter about basic business process knowledge. If patient safety and management system topics are new to you, I recommend reading the chapters in sequence, to get insights into what a management system is, in conjunction with patient safety, and what support can be expected of a management system in daily work. This book will introduce useful tools for designing a solid structure for a management system and for documenting processes within it, where the starting point is based on current safety research.

Using the Business Process Management Approach

In this book, the business process management approach is used selectively. Primarily, it is used in this book when forming structure for a management system. As a personal experience, when a management system reflects the business, it becomes easier to use, especially if it is organized according to the business processes.

Furthermore, the business process approach is used here to describe how to work with improvements toward increased patient safety. By visualizing the patients' journey through the healthcare system, important gaps and risks for information loss can be detected and addressed. The benefits on patient safety from having process-oriented management system have driven European legislation toward shaping management systems for health care in a business process-oriented way.

However, adopting these business process management aspects into health care does not imply considering health care as a standardized supply chain that can be optimized like a manufacturing industry. It is my firm opinion that health care cannot be regarded as such. It must be able to immediately adapt to prevailing circumstances and not be guided by any linear standard process. But at the same time, this cannot be the reason for refusing the whole package. There are advantages in the process approach that health care needs to take advantage of. The benefits include process diagramming that visualizes how we work, how we want to make work changes, where we can place indicators for quality measurements, and, not least, centering the improvements primarily to the benefits of the patients rather than to the organization structure.

CHAPTER 2

Safety and Patient Safety

Humans are also naturally adaptable and tend to improvise, which makes some non-compliance inevitable

—Carthey et al. (2011)

The aim of this chapter is to gain a common understanding about what safety and patient safety are and to give you insights into the ongoing paradigm shift in safety outlook from focusing on mistakes, to understanding why things run successfully. Safety scientists (Hollnagel 2014) indicate a need for a broader approach to safety management than the prevailing one. This new approach influences how to relate and how to manage patient safety matters, and can be put into practice in all aspects of patient safety work. One of the aspects is designing a management system. The purpose of a management system is to support the core operations, that is, the daily work done at the sharp end, next to the patient or care recipient, and to make more time available for performing safe health care instead of increasing administration for adverse events.

What Is Safety?

From the dawn of time when humanoid species started to develop, and thousands of years later, humans have been living under the continual threat of being either hurt or killed by animals or rival tribes. Despite considerably improved living conditions, humans still have a deep-rooted need to feel safe. This need is about being safe and above all, feeling safe. The insight into this profound need is important to remember and to understand, because it affects how we talk about safety, how we approach it, and how we manage it. The strife of human nature to satisfy that need has misled humans to seek for the simplest solutions, that is, to focus on what went wrong. This is a reactive behavior where the starting point is an adverse and unwanted event. The reason for focusing on what went wrong is that this is the easiest way to react to adverse events and to manage risks, because it gives humans a feeling of being safe and in control. Consequently, the key orientation to both safety and patient safety management is focusing on how to eliminate steps to these adverse events and trying to figure out how to prevent them from not happening again. Moreover, there is a tendency to make follow-ups on actions against the steps, which further lead to focusing on what went wrong. An additional aspect is looking at the costs of safety management in relation to "wrong" statistics and costs for its consequences.

The word safety is well known and appears in various contexts, for example, management systems, standards, documented procedures, research reports, or guidelines, but it is seldom or never defined or even explained. We humans just presume we are thinking and talking about the same thing. The lack of unitary definition is of course a problem, because it influences the approach to safety management, how it is measured, and what kind of steps are taken to action in order to achieve safety (Hollnagel 2014).

Safety has both emotional and physical attributes, and both must be in agreement for safety to be achieved. Patients know this all too well. From the moment a patient receives care, not only are the personnel devoted to ensure the emotional well-being of the patient, but they also dedicate themselves to protect the patient from experiencing harm. Kindness and compassion toward the patient may make a patient feel safe, but that alone is not enough to protect the patient from possible harm. On the other hand, a patient who is tucked safely in the hospital bed and well monitored may be physically safe from harm but may not feel safe if he or she doesn't understand the treatment plan.

Looking at how organizations or authorities define safety confirms that the focus mainly lies on errors, weaknesses, and mistakes. Some examples on how safety can be defined are presented next.

Safety is freedom from risk, which is not tolerable.[1] International Standard Organization (ISO)

---

[1] ISO/IEC Guide 51:2014, 3.14

Patient safety is protection from harm. Swedish Act on patient safety

Patient safety is the absence of preventable harm to a patient during the process of health care. World Health Organization (WHO)

Freedom from harm. The Leapfrog Group[2]

Freedom from harm or potential harm associated with healthcare. Institute of Healthcare Improvement (IHI)

Safety is the state of being certain that adverse effects will not be caused by some agent under defined conditions.[3]

These definitions are quite similar, and the absence of harm is one way or another a starting point. The last one also includes a state of being, in other words a feeling. Safety scientists like professor Hollnagel define this kind of approach as Safety-I (Hollnagel, Wears and Braithwaite 2015). When safety management is described, designed, and executed using Safety-I approach, the focus is then on finding and investigating the amount of undesired or adverse events. The methodologies used are root-cause analysis, occurrence analyses, and a countless numbers of aberration reports. For example, to support this, all the personnel in Sweden,working in health care, taking care of the elderly or taking care for people with disabilitys, have a legal obligation to write aberration reports. The work with patient safety matters has its starting point in outlook of Safety-I. Safety-II is an complementary approach and is defined, among others, by professors Hollnagel, Wears, and Braithwaite (2015). This outlook has its focus on understanding what went right and was successful. It aims to achieve as high score as possible of successful and acceptable outcomes.

In conclusion; the focus of Safety-I is on looking at failures of the past, while that of Safety-II lies in understanding successes of the past and in current work-as-done which is one of the characteristics of high-reliability organizations (HROs). HROs not only strive for effective

---

[2] From e-mail conversation with Leapfrog Group

[3] https://thefreedictionary.com/safety

standardization of healthcare processes, but go far beyond standardization and are described as "a condition of persistent mindfulness within an organization, where resilience is cultivated by relentlessly prioritizing safety over other performance pressures" (Chassin et al. 2013).

The Patient Safety Paradigm Shift

Without changing our patterns of thought, we will not be able to solve problems we created with our current patterns of thought
—Albert Einstein

Safety-I: In Other Words, What Went Wrong

Looking back in history, safety management development has its roots in the United States, side by side with the development of the industrial revolution when building constructions, machines, and infrastructure were built as never before. From about 1760 to 1840, the transition from hand production to new manufacturing processes began. Industries grew and people began to operate machine tools, steam power, and technical equipment. Consequently, new professions and workplaces developed, and new risks occurred. The first federal law regarding safety was founded on March 2, 1893. Enactment of *The Safety Appliance Act*[4] made air brakes and automatic couplers mandatory on all trains in the United States. The law took effect in 1900, after a seven-year-long grace period, and it was credited with a sharp drop in accidents on American railroads in the early 20th century. Demands for being profitable brought more actions against aberrations, since these led to delays resulting in high costs. Human power soon became compared to machines, but was described as slow, defective, and unreliable. A human could make mistakes, while machines kept on going with repeatable results.

Scientists such as mechanical engineer Fredrick Winslow Taylor began to search for explanation models to understand how errors occurred. He wanted to prevent aberrations and to make humans work as efficiently as machines. In 1911 Taylor summed up his efficiency techniques in his

---

[4] https://en.wikipedia.org/wiki/Railroad_Safety_Appliance_Act

book *The Principles of Scientific Management* and soon his management methodologies became famous worldwide. Consequently, safety management in industry developed from his work. Professor Hollnagel (2014) argues that management of patient safety in health care today is still strongly influenced by the safety approach from the industry sector which was developed and set in stone somewhere between1965 and 1985, when the complexity and demands of work were very different from today's. According to Hollnagel, the main assumptions of safety matters still are that

- "Systems and places of work are well-designed and correctly maintained.
- Procedures are comprehensive, complete, and correct.
- People at the sharp end (operations) behave as they are expected to, and as they have been trained to. (They work as they are supposed or imagined to.)
- Designers have foreseen every contingency and have provided the system with appropriate response capabilities. Should things go completely wrong, the systems can degrade gracefully because the operators can understand and manage the contingencies."[5]

These premises have unfortunately been adopted into complex environments, for example, hospitals, without any further consideration (Hollnagel 2014). Up to now a broad research and vast development of different medical specializations have resulted in a dramatic development of health care and the demands on personnel working with it. Numerous new diagnostic methods, high-technological equipment, new medical professions and specialties, new and advanced treatments, new drugs, highly narrow specialized care units, and much more have been developed. All together the complexity has increased vastly and has been followed by more new risks. These risks must be managed by new safety approaches rather than by the old ones.

Since the1970s, as part of developing operation, different approaches have been developed and are still being used to manage the growing complexity in health care. The healthcare administrators work very hard with

---

[5] Hollnagel, E., R.L. Wears, and J. Braithwaite. 2015. p. 11.

quality documents, root-cause analysis, LEAN, standards, guidelines certifications, and so on. Based on a belief that causes stand in proportion to outcomes, most methods and tools to manage patient safety presume predictability and inherent linear relationships. Using these methods has become common, resulting in solving problems by:

- Telling personnel and managers to work a little bit harder and to think smarter
- Writing new procedures
- Recommending more rigorous procedures
- Demanding more thorough reporting of errors
- Authorities demanding broader reports
- Requiring more resources

In consequence, safety work is triggered when a patient has been harmed. This is a reactive approach, resulting in undesirable events occurring since something has gone wrong. Therefore, the arguments imply that undesirable results also have reasons, which can also become identified and dealt with. Accordingly, all accidents are preventable. That is the main reason for accident analyses, searching for missing links and weaknesses in activities, and the analysis determines the probability of whether the same accident could happen again.

A major quality initiative covering many hospitals in the United States started in the 1980s by introducing total quality management (TQM), found by Eduard Deming, a management consultant whose work had a great impact on Japanese manufacturing. Deming helped post-World War-II Japan to improve their industry and economy, by shifting focus from profit to quality. He based his framework on three principles: continuous improvement, customer focus, and teamwork. While TQM became a great success for Japanese industry, when adopted by health care, it turned out not always to be as successful, mainly because of insufficient support given to healthcare professionals, a lack of leadership commitment, and a lack of pervasive TQM-based strategy for implementing the TQM in the organization at all levels (Hanna and Sethuraman 2005). Moreover, the existence of many powerful subcultures within health care worked against weak psychological safety. TQM's main focus is on ensuring that internal guidelines and process standards reduce errors, which actually is in alignment with Safety-I, and despite great efforts in achieving patient safety, improvements are not as big as expected. Most managers running healthcare organizations attribute human unreliability to undesired variability. As a consequence, the safety management mainly strives to eliminate risks as far as possible.

Another common way to relate to safety management is to focus on combinations of errors and random conditions that could create unexpected risks. An explanation for the process of failure was offered by James Reason (1997), professor at the University of Manchester, who presented a graphical model of how accidents could be seen, the so-called *Swiss cheese model* (SCM). Professor Reason explained safety management through the metaphor of Swiss cheese slices, as layers of different safety barriers aimed to prevent adverse events occurring. The cheese slices represented these barriers at different levels, such as organizational, technical, cultural, and individual. In the ideal world, the barriers were supposed to be robust and well heeled. When something unexpected happened, some of the barriers were supposed to stop the unwanted process and thereby prevent harm. Unfortunately, weaknesses could emerge on every level and risks for harm occurred, because the barriers could be influenced by people's conscious choices and random presumptions. If weaknesses at every step of the process emerged and the barriers failed, harm to a patient would then occur. Despite being a touch of a systemic view, the SCM is no longer applicable in today's advanced health care. One of the reasons is that the context of modern health care can no longer be explained using simple linear methods. So, are there complementary approaches and analysis methods for safety management? The next section shortly presents how scientists today are looking at safety by showing an alternative way to manage and achieve patient safety.

Safety-II: Understanding When Things Go Right

Let us for a moment go back to humankind's original life conditions, when life was a struggle to survive hunger, weather, dangerous animals, and diseases. One of the keys to our species' survival was our ability to adapt to various conditions, despite being neither the fastest, nor the strongest species. Although many thousands of years have passed since human footprints were found on Africa's coasts, we are still in possession of this essential ability to adapt. We use it daily, more or less consciously, for example, when driving a car, navigating relationships with other people, or when decisions are to be made fast.

The main outlook for Safety-II is that variation is natural, and it appears in all contexts. Consequently, the context of daily work demands our ability to adapt to the ongoing variations in workflow. Safety is described in terms of what happens when safety is present, thus not an absence of risk or harm. In other words, safety is about understanding what happens when things go right. The proportion between the number of events with unacceptable outcomes makes approximately 2 percent of every-day actions, exceptional performance makes another 2 percent, and in between there is 96 percent of day-to-day performance with acceptable outcomes (Hollnagel, Wears, and Braithwaite 2015). This means that this broad field between disaster and excellence can provide all personnel, involved in work with patient safety, with shared knowledge, experience, and solutions based on the best practice. Above all, it is available on a daily basis, thanks to people's ability to adapt to various conditions, to think abstractly, to express ideas, to connect, and to create a space for learning and trust.

Health care has a lesson to learn from HROs, where it is recognized that human variability in the shape of compensations and adaptations to changing conditions represents one of the system's most important safeguards (Dekker 2018). Industries like commercial aviation, offshore platforms, nuclear power plants, or amusement parks, which operate under hazardous conditions while maintaining high safety levels, are examples of HROs. The healthcare business is often compared to these industries but is rarely as successful in managing safety matters. Weick and Sutcliffe described HROs way of staying safe as "collective mindfulness" where all staff look for, and report, small problems or unsafe conditions before they pose a substantial risk to the organization and while they are easy to fix. One of the most prominent characteristics of a HRO's mindset is not being satisfied with whatever the current level of safety might be. The managers and the staff are always looking for new ways to continuously improve safety. The Joint Commission Center for Transforming

Healthcare defines high reliability as "consistent excellence in quality and safety across all services maintained over long periods of time." The commission has recognized three components for robust process improvement (RPI®). These are LEAN, six sigma, and change management. All these tools supported by the philosophy of LEAN and systemic approach of change management are seen as complementary and providing the best available methods for healthcare organizations to achieve major improvements in processes when used together.

Safety-II focuses on humans' and organizations' resilience and ability to maintain organizations' processes and operations, both when everything goes as per plan and when unexpected events occur. It means that the organization and people working within it are able to manage the daily tasks under both usual and unexpected conditions. The linear cause–effect thought process is replaced by a broader approach looking at the vast number of successful events. When the outcome is a mishap, then the explanations lie in understanding that there are transitory and temporary factors in the same broad field, where successful and unsuccessful work is done. Richard Cook, professor in patient safety at KTH, Royal Institute of Technology in Sweden, at his speech at a patient safety conference in Lund, Sweden, encouraged to "look for the things going right instead of wrong, and enforce knowledge and teamwork at the work floor."

Safety-II focuses on what went right, which happens most of the time, and offers keys to success in the daily work of personnel at the sharp end. This is exactly the starting point a management system should have, meaning the processes described in the management system should be describing *work as done*. The managers at all levels must create space and time for multiprofessional discussions, exchange of experiences, and learning and development of best common practice together (Törner et al 2013).

Sharing common knowledge also creates awareness of which behaviors, procedures, and processes need to be adjusted or changed to promote patient-safe performance. It creates a proactive mindset allowing personnel to react and act when risks or need for education show up. Others working at the office desk far away from the operative work cannot carry out such descriptions of processes and procedures. When they do, the procedure descriptions reflect work as imagined or prescribed, but not as it is performed in reality.

Table 2.1 shows basic differences between the Safety-I and Safety-II outlook.

Table 2.1 Basic difference between Safety-I and Safety-II

	Safety-I	**Safety-II**
Outlook on safety	Avoiding mishaps so that as few things as possible go wrong	Assuring that as many things as possible go wright
Principles on safety management	Reactive to something that have happened	Proactive and continuously trying to retrieve knowledge of successful outcomes
View of the personnel	personnel are seen as unreliable and making mistakes	personnel are seen as organizations most important resource, necessary for creating flexibility and resilience of the system
Adverse event investigation outlook	To identify the causes as accidents are seen as a result of malfunction and failures	Success and accidents happen in the same range of activities. The investigation focuses on understanding how things usually go right and use this understanding as a base when trying to explain how things occasionally go wrong
Evaluation of risk	Since accidents are seen as a result of malfunction and failures, the investigation focuses on finding causes and contributory factors.	To understand the ongoing conditions in cases where variability can become hard or even impossible to monitor and consequently impossible to control

It is important to remember that it is neither the one outlook nor the other. Both are needed. However, the Safety-I approach is the only line of reasoning which does not apply any more to modern safety management. Safety researchers suggest using a new pair of glasses when looking for new solutions to old and expensive problems.

Despite enormous attempts nationally and internationally, poor patient safety has not decreased. When we make an effort to increase things to go well, instead of decreasing things going wrong, then unlimited opportunities emerge. Vast improvements can be made in small steps every day on a broad basis creating a noticeable impact, compared to reactive actions based on relatively few events. Here comes my definition of safety.

Safety is an ongoing dynamic state where as much as possible goes right.

The state depends on interface between political, organizational, socio-psychological, technical, and individual preconditions.

Safety is, therefore, much more than absence of risk.

"Focus on what goes right as well as learning from what goes wrong" was one of six "resolutions" presented at IHI's National Forum in December 2016. It was followed by moving to greater proactivity; creating systems for learning from learning; being humble, in other words, building trust and transparency; coproducing safety with patients and families; and finally recognizing that safety is more than the absence of physical harm—it is also the pursuit of dignity and equity (Frankel et al. 2017).

Reliability is in Safety-II defined as a *dynamic nonevent*. It is dynamic meaning that safety is preserved by timely performed human adjustments, and it is a nonevent because successful outcomes rarely call attention to themselves.

Chapter Summary

This chapter has presented a brief overview of Safety-I and Safety-II outlooks on safety management. Humans have a deep-rooted need to feel safe, but the feeling of being safe doesn't automatically imply real safety. Thus, the many attempts made to block the various risks, based on knowledge about mistakes from the past, have proven not to be enough. The safety science suggests a more proactive approach, explaining variation as natural and existing in all contexts. It is also acknowledged as one of the system's most important safeguards. Thanks to people's instantaneous ability to make decisions when unexpected events occur, many accidents and disasters have been avoided, for example, "Miracle on the Hudson" described in the news as "the most successful ditching in aviation history." Safety is explained in terms of what happens when safety is present, in other words when things go right.

Patients and their families anticipate health care to be free from complication-related matters. They expect high quality and accessibility at a reasonable cost. Hence safety should not be regarded as absence of failures. Personnel should not be satisfied by just blindly following regulations and laws. Healthcare organizations and care providers can't just offer a feeling of safety. What they can do, among other important things, is to create as much clarity, structure, and support as possible, without designing rigid systems demanding total compliance. Management systems should be designed and filled with content not only for managers but for personnel within all professions and at all levels who work at the sharp end. The purpose of the management system from this point of view is to make it easier to do things correctly and to minimize bureaucracy by cleaning out heavy procedural deposits and promoting communication across organizational or economical boundaries. Hence working with health care should be designed to facilitate doing things as right as possible and understanding why.

The following chapter will introduce the concept of management system, designed to give support in the daily work for those who create patient safety at the sharp end and therefore mirroring *work as done*.

CHAPTER 3

What Is a Management System?

In order to create a given place for a management system in a daily work routine, first you have to understand what it is, how it works, and how it can support daily work at the sharp end. When you have accessed the knowledge of how a management system can benefit you, you can also decide on its design and content. Only then can the management system become a support for all personnel who pursue patient care safety, regardless of the organizational level they are working on.

Management System Definition

A management system is a structure for describing work as done in a workplace, on all organizational levels, in an organized and systematic way, based on a set of principles. The management system for patient-safe health care is aimed to provide managers and personnel at the sharp end with reliable support in their daily work, to promote psychological safety. The overall aim of the system is to increase patient safety and patient satisfaction.

My definition of a management system corresponds to the Safety-II approach. It mirrors work as done on a daily basis, and not work as imagined or prescribed by someone working far away from the demands of operational reality. The International Organization of Standards (ISO) describes management systems as a "way in which an organization manages the inter-related parts of its business in order to achieve its objectives."[1]

A management system is often seen as a set of policies, processes, and procedures used by managers to set objectives and to measure effects, to ensure the fulfillment of the tasks required to achieve organization's

---

[1] https://iso.org/management-system-standards.html

objectives. These objectives should cover many different aspects of the organization's operations, for example, product quality, client relationships, safety management, worker management, or financial outcomes. The bigger the organization, the greater the complexity. Therefore, the management system should contain descriptions of core operations, for example, taking care of patients, and the supportive processes, for example, administration, HR, IT, cleaning services, and supplies, into account. Management systems are also a resource of maintaining quality.

- *Management*: Act as a guide to managers working in the organization and coordinate their efforts toward the attainment of the common objective by planning the operations, organizing activities, resources, and staffing, and ensuring that right people are appointed to the right job, directing, for example, guiding and supervising, or making sure that staff performance is in alignment with the organizational goals.
- *Leadership*: A process of social influence, which maximizes the efforts of others toward the achievement of a goal.[2]
- *Continuous improvement*: An ongoing effort to improve products, services, or processes.
- *Development of processes*: Improving an organization's way of working by identifying and creating the most efficient processes that bring the best results for the receiver of the process.
- *Development of procedures*: Improving instructions or steps that describe how to complete a task or do a job.
- *Monitoring*: Process that helps improve performance and achieve results in project management.

Using this outlook, the management system for patient-safe care becomes a collection of tools supporting healthcare processes when delivering safe treatment and care to the receivers of process outcomes, that is patients. The core operations are, for example, all the activities providing the immediate health care in a hospital. In other words, the core business/

---

[2]   https://forbes.com/sites/kevinkruse/2013/04/09/what-is-leadership/ #670805745b90

process is the main reason for going to work, where the value for the patients is created and delivered. The concept of a management system is built upon two words: *management* and *system*. Before looking at how to develop, use, and maintain the management system, let us create a common picture of what these words mean, starting with *management*.

Management is (among other things) about the activities of an organization or business in order to achieve defined objectives. It means defining objectives, providing necessary resources, managing the resources in the best possible way, and hopefully also achieving the objectives.

The second word is *system*. Imagine a human cell. It is defined by the cell membrane as the outer boundary. Inside there is cytoplasm, organelles, and genetic material. Analogous to the different organs inside a human body, the organelles are adapted and/or specialized for carrying out one or more vital functions of the cell. For the cell to function correctly, all the organelles need to function as designed. There is a clear purpose of the system, depending on the function in the organism, for example, to trigger an electrical impulse in a heart muscle cell or to transport oxygen molecules to other cells or to produce gastric acid. If there is damage in the cell organelles and the cell is malfunctioning, the whole organ, and thus the whole organism, becomes affected. The single parts are connected, and the function of the whole is dependent on the function of the parts. Separated, they are not a system and interactions are required for designated functions.

An organization can be compared to a human cell or an organism consisting of many cells. It has a purpose and consists of different parts that depend on cooperating. This cooperation, unlike the cells, occurs in order to achieve organizational objectives. An organization is an entity comprising people, and it has a particular purpose. It can be an institution, an association, a business, or fellowship.

The healthcare sector has become a complex sociotechnical system, which involves many different sections that need to cooperate when creating safe health care for the patients. Variation is natural and exists in all contexts and, as you have learned, is one of the system's most important safeguards. Therefore, the management system needs to be systematically updated in order to keep procedures and standard practices mirroring *the work as done*. It is wise to reflect on the possibility that the work undertaken could be unsafe, as was the case when doctors didn't wash their hands between performing postmortems and delivering babies. My point is that the doctors did not discuss why many mothers died postpartum and why some survived, so they did not understand why they had failed or why they had succeeded. When there is time scheduled and psychological safety is present, the experiences are shared, and a vast amount of information and knowledge is relayed back to the healthcare staff and a good circle of ongoing improvements emerge.

This is one of the core steps of TQM. When not being truly implemented, continuous improvement fails. To be honest that is not how most medical systems really work, as they are much more focused around physician schedules and not the patient's path through the healthcare system.

The management system, designed the way I have recommended, provides

- More distinct operational management with fact-based decisions
- Structure that brings order and makes it easier to find relevant information
- A greater share of common agreed (standardized) work procedures
- Increased patient safety
- Increased traceability of what is going on in the organization, when and how
- A drive for continuous improvement, by creating transparency and ownership of the outcome and benefits of the processes
- Shared knowledge becoming common practice
- Decreased waste and increased economic outcomes

Examples of what a management system contains:

- Documents
- Web-based text and figures
- Instruction films

The management system content can comprise/describe/visualize

- Organizational objectives, for example, "20% more complication free hip and knee surgeries" or "improving the start time in the operating room by 50%"
- Policies, for example, code of privacy, dress code, non-smoking policy
- Quality parameters, for example, time from referral to diagnosis, numerical value for malnutritional risk, decreased prescription of antibiotics
- Guidelines on operational follow–up—how to report and manage operational quality and objectives
- Descriptions of positions, roles, and responsibilities
- How the operations run—process and procedure descriptions of work as done
- How to manage continuous improvement and how to retrieve experiences and knowledge to the organization making improvements real in the daily schedule
- How to manage aberrations
- How to manage, update, and maintain the management system for patient-safe care

Summarizing all the above-mentioned items, you could say that the management system describes

- Organizational objectives
- Who is responsible for what
- How to achieve the objectives
- How to manage certain situations
- How to monitor the objectives in order to know if we are on the "right path"

In parallel, the management system has another important purpose. This is to promote continuous improvement by giving direct support to the personnel in their daily work, by creating a robust, trustworthy, and an "easy to navigate" structure for necessary procedure descriptions, instructions, and other important information, created by those who perform the work and consequently describing the work as done.

A broad structure of a management system may look as follows:

- *How to manage, lead, and develop an organization, concerning*
  - Operational management
  - Policies and guidelines
  - Operational development
  - Aberration report management
  - Safety management
  - Environment management
  - Project management
  - Communication strategies
  - Requirement management
  - Emergency management
  - Quality management
- *How to operate the core operations, explained in*
  - Procedures descriptions
  - Instructions
  - Technical descriptions and manuals
- *The necessary prerequisites needed and how to use them, regarding*
  - Personnel and competence provision, that is, planning for current and future recruiting, educating, and training of the personnel
  - Work environment management
  - Creating and measuring the culture
  - Strategy for leadership
  - Material supply and services management, for example, IT support, cleaning services, food services, transport services, procurement management, HR management
  - Documentation and archiving, principles and templates for different kinds of documents, archiving instructions

Almost every above-mentioned part of the management system can be described by mapping the process, thus by creating step-by-step descriptions of *how the work is done.* When orientated toward a process, a management system becomes more resilient to reorganizations and easier to maintain and to keep vivid (Ljungberg and Larsson 2012). It is natural for dynamic environments and organizations to reorganize, but it doesn't automatically mean that the structure of a management system has to be changed.

If you need to quickly measure "the temperature" of your management system, use this checklist to ask your managers and staff whether the following statements are true:

Our management system
- Makes it easy for personnel to find required information
- Describes by its content, *work as done*
- Meets the regulatory requirements
- Is patient and process orientated
- Promotes systematic improvements of work, procedures, and patient safety
- Contributes to creating a learning organization

If some of the items are missing, there is room for improvement. In order to create a robust skeleton-like structure for your management system, the next chapter will give you the basics of business process mapping with some practical hints on how to get started. When that has been done, we'll get back to designing a management system.

CHAPTER 4

Business Processes Fundamentals

Process theories became apparent at the beginning of the 1990s as a way of improving quality, getting costs under control, and increasing through-put in manufacturing industries. These ideas also became accessible to the information and service sectors, as well as to health care. The main driving force for the process-outlook focuses on the customer/receiver of the process outcomes. In reference to health care, it means adapting workflow to the patient, care receiver, resident, and their families. The first thing to do is to identify and to describe processes. In other words, to graphically show and describe, with text, work as done. The complete process descriptions, roles and function descriptions, clearly explain who does what by using step-by-step operation descriptions. This chapter explains how to draw and describe processes in a clear and useful way.

Process Definition

Let's start by defining the concept, *process*. According to the Oxford living dictionary,[1] a process is a "series of actions or steps taken in order to achieve a particular end." This definition contains some important key words:

- *Series of actions*. A process is expressed by an aggregation of activities. Looking at an example from daily life such as going to the grocer's and buying food, you will immediately identify several steps in that process: making your way to the store, picking up your articles, paying and making your way home.

---

[1] https://lexico.com/en/definition/process

The "buying food" event fulfills process definition because it contains several activities.

- *Achieving a particular end.* A process has a defined and noticeable outcome. It should be possible to know whether a process is completed or not. When buying food, you will easily notice if that is the case.

Ljungberg[2] expands the definition by adding a very important key word:

Process is a repetitively applied network with orderly linked activities, using information and resources, starting from evident need in order to create the value which satisfies the need.

The key word is *repetitively.* This means that the same process can be done many times by the same or different personnel, regarding the same or different patients. Another process attribute, worth mentioning, is that it often crosses organizational boundaries. A process may start at one unit, pass through others and finally end somewhere else. For example a patient becomes ill at home, arrives at emergency unit (EU), gets CT-scanning, receives care at a ward, has surgery done in the operating theater, goes through rehabilitation, and finally receives care at an elderly people's home. This kind of scenario makes the healthcare process perspective complicated but at the same time exciting as it creates new workflows and gives room for many improvements.

Now we are going to add another key word to the definition: *a process is initiated by an event.* This means that there is a clear trigger, starting the process. In the example in Figure 4.1, *Perform surgery on patient*, we can easily see that the process is initiated by a patient arriving at an outpatient-surgery reception.

The definition for the concept of "process" is very important as it affects our mental picture of the event we want to describe. If we regard the process approach as a means for transformation aimed for internal effectiveness, the focus will turn to mapping and improving, aimed "only" to strengthen the quality and make the process more effective.

If instead we understand and embody the process as value-creating activities received by the customer of the process outcome, then we have a

---

[2] Ljungberg, A., and E. Larsson. 2012. p. 60

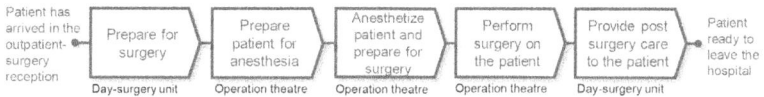

Figure 4.1 Process perform surgery on patient containing distinct defined steps and with clear criteria for initiation and outcome of the process

very different view. What does that view mean in practice? To begin with, "customer-oriented" becomes replaced by "patient-oriented." Patient orientation implies a broader process approach rather than focusing on one unit at a time. Picture an elderly person, who is living in a care setting, arriving at an EU. The process starting point is traditionally the arrival at the EU. Using a patient-oriented approach, the process had already started when the patient was discovered in a bad condition and needing care at EU. The first step had already taken place at the care setting. This patient-oriented process is not fulfilled until that patient returns to normal life again.

In other words, many different providers and professionals may be engaged in the patient's process. A truly patient-oriented process approach implies that there are full insights and awareness of how the patient's needs are fulfilled, even if the patient's journey crosses organizational stovepipes and economic governance.

Describe Processes in a Useful and Clear Way

There are several reasons why process descriptions should be created. My point in picking up the subject is mainly to give you a foundation when you are about to form processes, to create a skeleton-like structure for your management system. Another use of describing processes might be when

- *Explaining how the work functions.* Process descriptions provide other stakeholders with important insights, for example, to clarify the interface between cooperating businesses or partners. Moreover, the process descriptions can be used when communicating implementation requirements for the organization, management system, and IT systems.
- *Improving operations.* In order to do a better job by increasing the quality and patient satisfaction, saving time and resources,

it is a very good idea to visualize how the work is done today. It gives you an opportunity to compare with others, find possible improvements, and to work in a new way in the future.

- *Managing and following up the work.* Many different organizations have chosen to organize their processes and therefore need process maps so that they can allocate accountability, distribute resources, and design a structure for follow-ups.

Many people experience a process outlook as easy to understand and operation processes easy to create. This simplicity in understanding is one of the advantages, but it is also a mind trap. You might get deceived and create unusable results and outcomes when modeling processes by believing it is easily made, without any knowledge of how to do it. To prevent this trap, this chapter is going to give you basic ideas about drawing processes followed by some other hints and suggestions for how to organize the work aiming to create process descriptions.

Symbols and Process grammar

Learning some useful symbols when reading or drawing processes is the right place to start. Let us have a closer look at the *Perform surgery on patient* process. In Figure 4.2 you can see all the components of a process:

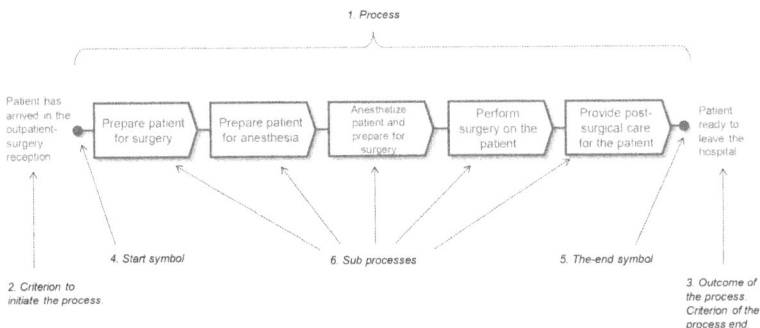

Figure 4.2 Example of a process, explaining different parts of a process map

1. The process. The whole picture from left to right describes the process.

2. The starting criterion or starting event for the process. It is important to keep in mind that it should not contain any kind of information or material coming into the process. What is of interest is the event starting the process.

3. The outcome and the ending criterion of the process. Both the starting events and the outcomes should be clear and measurable.

4. Symbol indicating start of the process.

5. Symbol indicating the end of the process.

6. Subprocesses composing steps in the process. Each of the subprocesses can contain its own description and can sometimes consist of its own steps. Altogether, the subprocesses create results of the process. Subprocesses are drawn as arrow-ended graphical symbols (in Sweden, called process-fish symbols).

It is easy to become fooled when you look at a document and see it as an input for a process, and to see the same or another document as the output of the process after it has been completely handled. Thinking this way usually results in depicting the ongoing document flow and omitting the vital value-adding activities in the process diagram. There are examples when a process initiation is described as an "action plan." Such a description is very vague, raising questions such as: What state should the action plan be in? Does it need to be decided? Does it need to be communicated? A better example would be to express a clear criterion that can initiate the process such as "decided action plan is ready to be executed."

Connecting the processes with a line is a way to visualize the steps being both connected and making it complete. In some cases, arrows are used instead of plain connection lines. Drawing an arrow indicates mandatory connection between activities. In health care, the order of activities usually varies greatly. Therefore, it is good practice to cover what activities are included in the process, rather than determining a certain order they must occur in.

In real life, variations of activity order usually occur. Using the arrow-ended process symbol implies a movement from left to right.

When naming the process, I recommend you use simple "grammar rules":

- Imagine there is a "to" written before the process name: *to* make shopping, *to* perform surgery, *to* prepare for anesthesia. Writing this way gives the reader a feeling of rhythm and vitality in description.
- Always write both verb and subject when naming the process. It is not enough to just write "plan" as a process name. Those who are going to read this must know what is going to be planned, for example, plan for treatment evaluation.

Now you have accessed the basics in process mapping, making it easier to create friendly-to-read process descriptions. Let's put it into practice and make some drawings.

Draw Process Map

Processes describing the operations at an overall level and having an external customer are called main processes. In turn, main processes consist of subprocesses that together create value. This value should be perceived by the receiver of the main process's outcome, for example, the patient. That is where patient satisfaction can be monitored by simply asking the patient. Regardless of the process level, it can be described by the graphical arrow symbol (process-fish). A diagram containing processes is called a process map. The following steps are useful when creating a process map:

1. Begin by deciding the purpose of the process map. It helps when deciding phrases, extent of detail, and the boundaries for the process.
2. Continue by deciding what is the expected end result of the process and who is the direct receiver of its outcome. The process map should always clearly show who is the receiver of the value created by the process.
3. The next step is to determine the start. It is easier to do that when the end result is defined. In other words, what kind of event initiates the main process and each subprocess. If the receiver is an external

party, then the starting event should also be external. It may be of help to think "from arisen need, to fulfilled need." Such a sequence of processes connected end-to-end forms a *value chain*.

4. Place the starting event to the left of the process map and the outcome at the right wing.

5. Now identify processes between the left and right wings. Work with one chain at a time. Ask yourself if there are some important subresults between the starting event and the outcome. You may find 3 to 20 subresults, depending on a demarcation of the process. Try to create one process per outcome in order to have a true picture of the operation.

6. Create names according to rules you gained in the previous part. Name-giving might be a challenge. By looking at the process outcome, you might get some help finding proper process names. If the process results in an action plan, you can name it "make an action plan."

Thus, start process mapping with enough broad scope to make sure that important activities, both before and after your organization, are included in the value chain. The value chain, shown in Figure 4.3, is described from an outpatient-surgery center's perspective. The value chain shows that a patient is in contact with a health center and specialist physician; these are activities before being a patient in the outpatient-surgery unit. You can also see that the patient may be provided postsurgery care, in a ward, at home, or not at all. Opportunities for seamless cooperations may emerge by clarifying the interfaces to surrounding processes.

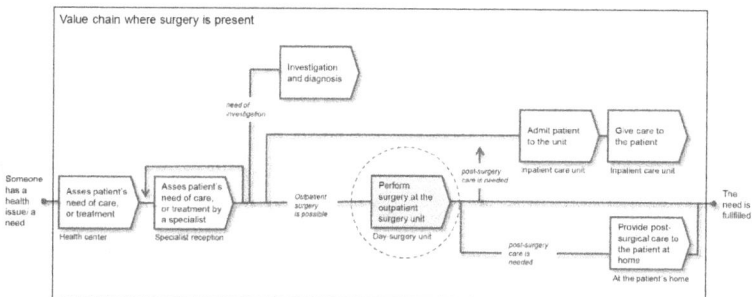

Figure 4.3 Value chain where perform surgery at outpatient-surgery unit is shown in its context

Process *Perform surgery at outpatient-surgery unit* needs to be described in a separate process map. This time it should be in more detail (lower process level) as shown in Figure 4.4.

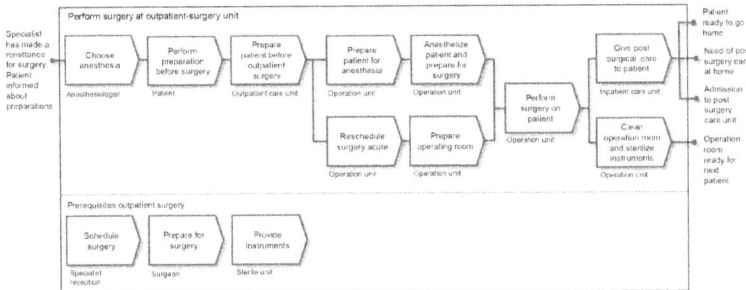

Figure 4.4 Process map describing processes within perform surgery at outpatient-surgery unit

The workflow is the same regardless of the detail level of the process map. Try not to take the organizational boundaries into account, since they are often subject to changes. Neither should you be tempted to let the IT-system form the demarcation. It is much better to follow partial results following patients' process. Identify the processes from the starting event on the left, working toward the outcome on the right wing. Tie the processes together with a line showing the flow. If you discover the process containing just one step, then I recommend placing that step in another process map. The most basic level of the process description is called *activity* and the next part will explain how to draw an activity diagram.

Draw Activity Diagram

An activity diagram is a model showing the process at its most basic level, meaning the process has reached its most detailed level and cannot be divided into smaller steps, at least not graphically. The example in Figure 4.5 shows one of the *Perform surgery at outpatient-surgery unit* processes described precisely in the activity diagram. Just as any process, at any level, it has a starting event and an outcome in the process description.

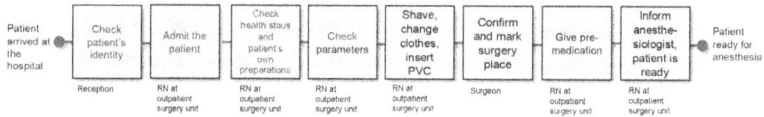

Figure 4.5 Activity diagram containing activities of perform surgery at outpatient-surgery unit process

An activity diagram consists of only one process and should have the same demarcation as the process it is describing (Figure 4.6).

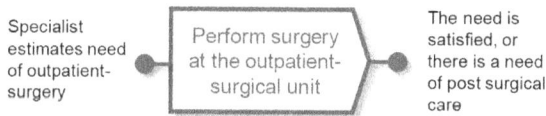

Figure 4.6 Demarcation for process is the same as for the activity-diagram

The activity in the diagram is graphically drawn as a square. Identify and phrase activities the same way as processes. In other words, imagine putting "to" in front of the verb followed by the subject. Name roles for those who usually perform activities and place the name right under the square. If there is an IT-system supporting the activity, put the name of the system above the square. Now you might ask yourself: How should I know how detailed the activity is? The rule of thumb when determining the level of an activity is as follows:

- Activity is mostly performed by one person without time gaps and at the same place.
- Activity can be performed manually, using some kind of system function, or completely by a system, for example, a phone call can coincide with activity.
- The following events are usually activities on their own:
  - Estimation or decision, for example, "decide on discharging patient" and "find out error cause."
  - New and important knowledge is picked up, for example, "get confirmation from medic" and "calculate dose."
  - A handgrip or procedure, for example, "insert PVC" (peripheral venous cannula) and "send referral to district nurse."

Avoid using performers' name or name of IT-system in the activity name. For example, "conversation with RN Annie" doesn't say what has been performed or what the result of the conversation was. It may be about more than one activity during the conversation. A better way to put it would be "check health status data and patient's own preparations." "Update Take Care" says neither about what is going on. It is much better to word the activity as "document changes in the drug list," "inform that the patient is ready for surgery." Place activities on a line in the sequence they are usually performed. Sometimes some activities are not always performed, depending on circumstances, but it is valuable to illustrate it. You can do so by drawing an arrow by-passing the unperformed activity. Always write down on the arrow line the reason for by-passing this particular activity or you can write it in text description, explaining the activity as not always cogent. The example in Figure 4.7 aims to illustrate that all patients will be prepared by shaving, changing clothes, and getting an intravenous cannula inserted, except for patients with special needs, for example, young children.

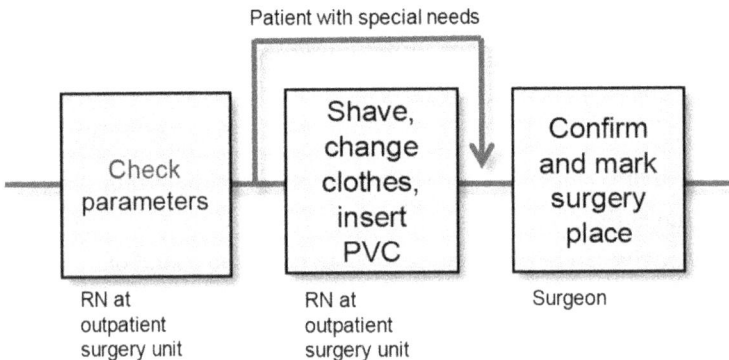

Patient with special needs

Check parameters	Shave, change clothes, insert PVC	Confirm and mark surgery place
RN at outpatient surgery unit	RN at outpatient surgery unit	Surgeon

Figure 4.7 How to draw arrow by-passing an activity in a process

It is quite usual that alternative ways emerge in a process. It happens when an outcome of a decision can result in the process taking different paths. How to draw alternative ways is illustrated in Figure 4.8 with lines showing two different paths to move the process forward.

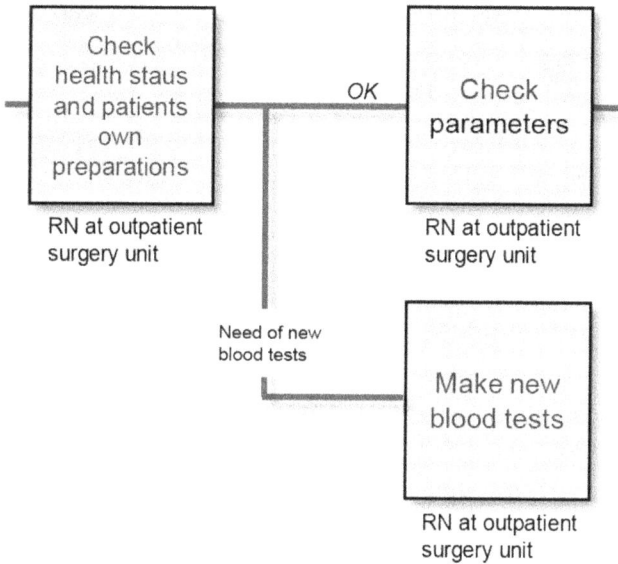

Figure 4.8 How to draw alternative ways of the process

With these few drawing variations, you can create complicated activity diagrams that are quite easy to read and understand. The same as Figure 4.5, but developed with alternative process ways, two starting events, and two alternative outcomes. Figure 4.9 shows an activity diagram with two different starting events, one possible by-pass of two activities, and a choice situation leading to two alternative process results. Together it makes five different variations of the same process.

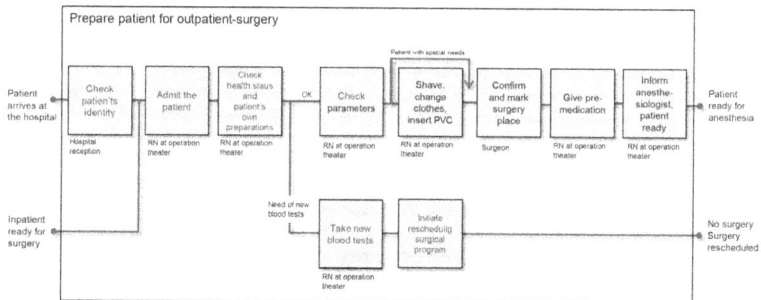

Figure 4.9 Activity diagram prepare patient for outpatient-surgery

The same as Figure 4.5, but developed with alternative process ways, two starting events, and two alternative outcomes.

Avoid expressing decisions as diamond symbols, which process syntaxes sometimes suggest. Decisions are activities in their own right and need to be documented properly. Diamonds in diagramming do not reflect decisions; they just reflect the outcomes from decisions. Skipping diamonds has been the best practice in business process management and among enterprise architecture professionals. Moreover, there are shortcomings using diamonds as they are restricted to just three possible outcomes whereas the reality has many more variations. Diamonds may work in simple diagrams aimed for computer programming, but not in a process-oriented management system.

Coming so far, it may be tempting to draw all the variations and possibilities for all different cases. Doing so risks having activity diagrams that are hard to read, understand, and maintain increases. Furthermore, it is basically impossible to exhaustively describe all the rules and exceptions. Rather keep the diagrams clean and write the exceptions in text. "Shave the patient, change patient clothes and insert intravenous cannula" may be done later to a patient with special needs, for example, a child, a person with mental health issues, or a person with disability. Thus, the activity can be described in a procedure description or with an arrow, showing the possibility of by-passing an activity in activity diagram.

A good rule to use is the "80–20 rule." The rule suggests you divide the process-mapping work into two parts. Start with modeling activities normally done in most of the cases, which is usually about 80 percent of the activities performed. Continue working on the remaining 20 percent including exceptions. Most of the time, the exceptions show to be unwanted variations depending mostly on insufficient prerequisites. That is the reason why in most cases it is enough to describe 80 percent of the scenarios and then work on improvements.

Document Processes and Activities

Process documentation should not stop with process-fishes, squares, and lines. There should also be a descriptive text. Regardless of describing a whole value chain, one process, or single activity, the description should contain

- The name of the process
- The starting event as well as the initiator of the process
- The outcome and who the receiver of the result is
- Who is performing the activity: a nurse, a doctor, an external party

- Text describing content of the process or activity
- Who has created the description and the date when it was done

The value chains can be described with objectives measures and frequencies, for example, how often the operation is performed. If the activity is described, the performer role and used IT-system may be written down in the document.

Processes at Different Levels

Three levels of a process are manageable (Figure 4.10). Making more levels in a management system makes it difficult to navigate and have an overview. You may have 15 to 20 processes per level and let the processes contain at least 7 subprocesses or activities. Otherwise there is a risk of building too many levels containing tiny processes. When described as recommended, you have the possibility of describing more than 3,000 activities.[3]

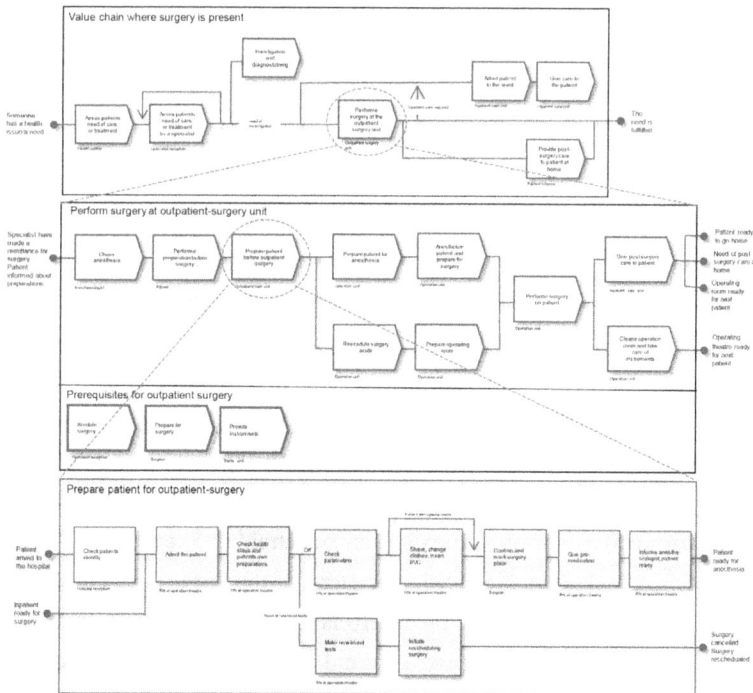

Figure 4.10 Process structure at three levels

---

[3]   A total of 20 processes, 7 subprocesses each, in 3 levels, 7 activities in each process = 2,940 activities and processes.

When the process is decomposed to a lower level, then the new level should have the same demarcation as its "parent-process," that is, the superior process. In the same way, the processes in the value chains should be connected, meaning that the outcome of one process should be a possible start event for the succeeding process. This is particularly important when process boundaries coincide with boundaries between two parties, for example, clinics, hospitals, care settings. Ensure the whole level structure is connected this way. Then, when new process descriptions are made, it will be possible to place these in the structure preventing new gaps.

Different Stakeholders in Process Chain

In a value chain of processes, there are always different stakeholders. There are those who are directly affected by the process, those who work within it; there are politicians, scientists, and the public, to mention some. How can we meet the different needs from such different interests in a process description? Start by considering those within the process and those close to it, for example, the receiver of the process outcome. The receiver is the person whose needs are the main purpose of the activities performed in the value chain. Except for the patient there are many other stakeholders contributing to or assisting the process— family members, front line managers, coordinators, or other people/ functions occurring later in the process, needing information on time, to progress the process smoothly. It is valuable to take these stakeholders into account when making process descriptions. It may appear as an activity, for example, making sure that special surgical instruments are available for a certain type of surgery, by making reconciliations or having an exchange of information between the hospital and healthcare facility.

Additionally, there are more distance stakeholders like personnel making follow-up reports, financial managers, authorities, media, and the public. As far as these are not the receivers of process outcomes on a daily basis, these types of stakeholders should be managed by creating processes, for example, "report to the CFO," "communicate to the media," "make quality follow-up," putting the stakeholders and outcome receivers in a more natural context.

Manage Process Gaps Between Stakeholders

As mentioned before, a value chain is a sequence of processes where the start and the end are placed outside your organization. Usually, the subprocesses have internal customers, for example, different units or wards in a hospital. But there might be external parties as well, like an elderly care setting or a remitting health center. Even though the different actors should have their own management systems, the stakeholders, that is, parties involved in the value chain, should agree on the entire chain of processes. This kind of cooperation and communication is required for avoiding gaps and overlaps in the value chain. Creating process descriptions together makes it easier to talk about the boundaries and gaps giving opportunities for improvement. Put some extra effort in working on activities close to the interface between the different parties as well as on elapsed time between activities in the process. Many operational problems, safety risks, and opportunities for improvement lie right in those interfaces. Many adverse events occur when important information is forgotten or lost.

If it is impossible to follow a patient's whole journey through the healthcare system, try at least to look back a couple of steps to the previous process, and also look a couple of steps forward into the connecting operation unit. This makes it easier to track down gaps and overlaps as well as to create awareness about the impact of current activities on the end result.

As I see it, the patient has an ethical, moral, and legal right to receive health care designed to deliver safety, security, continuity, care, and treatment, based on cooperation between all parties involved in the patient's process. There are many challenges in doing this, because processes usually pass through organizational and financial silo-like boundaries. Furthermore, new demands are made on managers who need an overview in order to provide the process with required resources.

If your organization is about to become process-oriented, then personnel at the sharp end should be provided with the necessary prerequisites to enable patient-oriented health care. Prerequisites include tools that enable the staff to be well aware of each patient's healthcare journey: where they come from, what their purpose is here and now, where they go next depending on the outcome, the requirements on each patient's journey in terms of urgency and timing to other activities, and so on.

The processes must start where the patient's need arise, follow a patient's whole healthcare journey and end, creating value for the patient and the patient's family.

Processes Management and Process Orientation

Done thoroughly, the process descriptions may be used in many ways. Of course, the mapping process makes a basic structure for the management system section, describing *how the work is done,* yet there are other areas of use such as:

- A starting point for operation development or/and process development
- A starting point for process-based monitoring
- A foundation for process-oriented management and control
- A foundation for creating culture of trust, psychological safety, and continuous knowledge exchange

Process development becomes operational development when looking over several processes and reflecting on:

- Whether all the activities are necessary
- Whether some activities may be performed by someone else, than today
- Whether it would be wiser to perform activities in a different sequence
- Whether all or some activities can be automatized by the IT-system

Regardless of whether your goal is to improve patient safety, enhance quality, or lower the costs, process development is an excellent way of achieving it. But remember, changing the organizational structure is not equivalent to developing processes; that is just revamping the existing processes and doesn't necessarily lead to desired improvements. Changing the organization in order to lower costs usually means that the same amount of work is to be carried out by fewer people.

When retaining or increasing the quality is the goal, professional process development is required. Developing processes gets easier when the starting point is understanding the current workflow. Then it is easier to discuss and see the difference between what reality looks like, and what kind of future is desired. Making the processes visible facilitates a development of procedures, management, and monitoring, helping to improve the entire value chain. I strongly recommend looking over the processes before using them as a structure for the management system.

Once the as-is process is documented and the expectations on future processes are determined, you can identify areas of improvements and come up with solutions that will meet those expectations, such as improved patient safety. Improvement could include best-practice activities, introducing check-ups, reorganizing materials, and standardizing procedures and denominations. Larger changes can include new equipment, computer systems, or even moving operations to other places.

Sometimes process changes are not necessary, as it may be enough to update the process description and let it reflect "work as done" in a way the co-workers recognize and agree to. Therefore, work in interdisciplinary groups using graphical maps. It gives the participants a possibility of getting instant feedback, and the results get much better using more than two- or four-eyes modeling processes.

The usual way to manage and measure operations is by following the hierarchical line organization. The executive management reporting is typically concentrated on monitoring the resources and spending, as they are anxious to understand "what do we get for our money." To report that, the accomplishments are typically measured, such as the visit volumes and other quantifiable turnouts. Quality measures are rare.

Process measurement is a complement to the traditional measures when following the process outcomes and performance. Then, the throughput can be measured by looking at how much time the whole value chain takes, from *arisen need to fulfilled need,* followed by looking at the waiting time and the end result. It may be crucial, for example, when tissue samples are taken suspecting cancer. The delay in getting test results may lead to delayed diagnosis and increased treatment actions. Another measurement to regard is the subjective side of the process such as customer satisfaction or customer's experiences. All together this gives quite a good picture of how well the process works. It also creates awareness about systemic dependencies within the organization when planning for reorganizations. Otherwise the risk of moving problems from one unit to another emerges. It is good to keep in mind that "despite of being aware of it or not, the value created on a daily basis is always performed in a process" (Roger Treager 2016).

In order to be process-orientated it is not enough to just describe processes. Neither is it enough to design the management system structure based on processes, or to implement process monitoring. To be truly process-orientated, the organization must live up to the above, and moreover to:

- Create accountabilities for forming processes in the right way and organizing process' prerequisites, especially equipment and knowledge
- Make sure that process objectives are defined and monitored and that someone has a mandate to initiate actions when objectives are not met
- Process management, develop processes, and continuously improve prerequisites

Consequently, the benefit of process orientation is having management concentrate on creating value for the receiver of the process outcome, that is, the patient. It is like putting on *from-outside-perspective-glasses* in order to catch the true process outlook at the ongoing operation. Using this perspective makes the activities and time gaps that don't bring value to the patients' needs obvious to the management. By extension, it results in reduced waste and more efficient use of both personnel and material resources in the organization. There is no fully process-oriented organization, but many have chosen process orientation covering customer-related processes while supporting functions are more traditionally managed. Figure 4.11 shows four steps of process maturity in organization.[4]

---

[4]   Process Orientation Maturity Model by Håkan Edvinsson and Per-Olof Graveleij, Informed Decisions Consulting AB

Organization
is process-
based

Process
management
structure is
created

Process
management
is applied

Organization
uses the
process
approach

*Processes are
described, known
and accurate.
Process goals are
defined and
measured.
Roles and
accountabilties are
appointed.*

*Senior management
requests process
measurement
outcome. Process
change responsibility
is appointed and
applied.
Improvements are
continously
implemented.*

*Silo organization has
ceased. Resource
owners are trusted
to maintain the
knowledge and the
proces's needs.*

*Business processes
are described.
May be used for
clarifying changes.*

Limited   Fair   Mature   Total

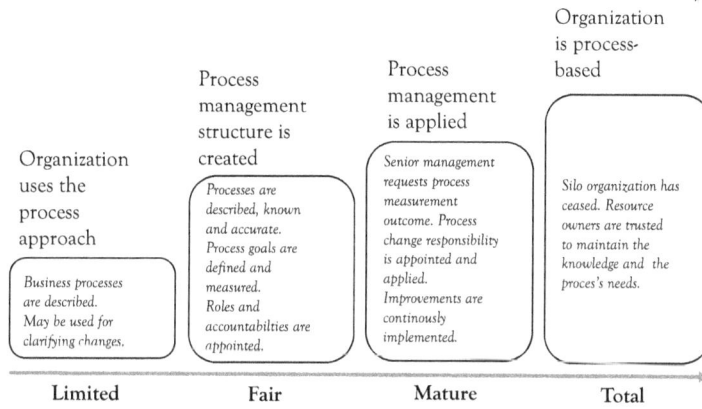

Figure 4.11 Process orientation maturity

The process orientation coincides with the Safety II outlook, teaching us that success lies in the ability to cope with ongoing variations, on a daily basis, to get the work done. In order to find out what we do, and to understand when things go right, we need to describe it in an easy-to-read and easy-to-understand way. Doing it with methodology and structure gives the opportunity of getting the same picture of reality and the ongoing processes throughout the process. Creating the same picture of realty gives room to create the necessary space for trust and functioning teamwork. Which step is your organization on, and where would you like to be?

CHAPTER 5

Designing a Management System

Previous chapters have referred to an outlook on patient safety through research development in this field. You have gained some basic knowledge about what a management system is and how to map a process properly. This chapter is an introduction to fundamental principles when designing a management system, and it gives some practical hints on how to get things done, how to implement, and how to maintain management system.

Like performing a symphony, it takes a lot of people working together to design and develop a management system. It is usually done as a project demanding highly skilled work, time, knowledge, engagement, and access to operational personnel. There may be a need to rebuild the entire structure of the management system or some parts of it or having different management systems integrated. Another possible scenario might be a need to redesign the current management system structure in order to improve operation processes with a view to increasing quality, strengthening patient safety, and getting finances in balance. The engagement and approval of top management is crucial to success. A lot of work should be done in seminars, that is, in a group working out the design and content of the management system. Basic presumptions for successful project outcome are:

- Solid sponsorship from operation management
- Engaged participation of representatives for operation, for example, nurses, doctors, technicians
- Experienced project and change management facilitators

In the following paragraphs, you'll find practical tips on how to plan the work on a management system project. The characteristic for working with patient safety improvement is the complexity due to different performers working together while delivering health care. Hence patient safety will never solely arise from updated instructions and role descriptions on their own; working on management systems also contains efforts on operational development.

Creating Prerequisites for a Successful Management System Project

When starting work on a management system it is important to get some essential preconditions in place. There must be a formalized decision from top management. That can be regarded as a starting point for a process to build a management system process. I'll walk you through it. When you are about to run such a process as a project, it is advisable you have the following questions answered by your project assigner:

- What are the delimitations for the project extent?
- Is a new management system about to be designed, or is the current one to be redesigned?
- How will the new management system relate to the existing ones, for example, how will they be integrated, or will this new management system replace the existing one?
- Is the management system to include the entire organization at all levels, or will it include only chosen parts, for example, core operations?
- What is the main driving force for the project, that is, why now? Typically, there are already decisions that have been made, for example, reorganizations or new ways of cooperation. It is important to know the driving forces behind those decisions, thus affecting project delimitations.
- What is the expected management system project outcome? Is it about lowering costs, increasing quality turn-out, that is, increased patient safety or reduced avoidable patient harm?
- Who is to receive project results while working on the project, and how is that role going to work based on the results?

The answers are crucial for designing the project, so it depends on what personnel and which competences are needed and on the planning time needed from the start to the implementation of the management system project. Another essential factor for a project's success and survival is true top management engagement and interest, for the project to result in strengthened patient safety. This kind of sincerity reflects in setting aside necessary time, showing engagement and giving resources for the work. Managers' important tasks are:

- Establishing a well-composed and engaged project group
- Granting necessary time to carry the project through
- Providing needed access to representatives for the operations and other necessary resources
- Having and maintaining a project plan

Since a management system project usually crosses organizational boundaries, the project process depends on strong support and sponsorship from top management. A sponsor with high credibility in the organization is vital for success and that person needs to be engaged and well informed in the value of a well-designed management system. The managers might have good insights into why the management system needs to be constructed or redesigned, but they seldom have the necessary knowledge on how the work should be done. Therefore, some opposing decisions may be taken jeopardizing the management system project. This insight puts great responsibility on the project managers/facilitators. They must keep the managers informed and engaged during the process to secure the desired project outcome. Meetings to report steps on the project should be kept interesting by showing examples that highlight the needs of the subproject by asking relevant and interesting questions to involved managers.

The extent of the management system and the size of the organization have an impact on organizing the project and deciding how many people should get involved. For example, if a health center manager has decided to improve the management system, then a possible scenario would be to engage a project manager who is experienced in mapping processes and to engage representatives from respective professions. A representative of top management should be invited to and present at the initial seminars, making him or her informed and engaged. Some of the seminars should be held together with representatives of external partners. If the purpose of the project is to create excellent care and patient satisfaction in the future, then representatives from different patient organizations and representatives of family members should also get involved in forming the to-be processes.

If we wish to extend our reasoning and apply it to a larger scale, for example, to a group of health centers run by the same owner, then the project could be run pretty much the same way as previously mentioned, but the need for shared knowledge of principles for designing, structure, content, and maintenance of the management system would rise. To make it work in real life, there should be staff designated to work by honoring the management system.

If the organization is large, for example, a hospital or several hospitals, other management representatives should get involved. In such a scenario it is also a good idea to put together a strategic group, consisting of managers, strategists, and other individuals who see new possibilities, who are driven by strong engagement, and who have powerful visions for the future of the organization. Such a group will have the possibility of maintaining room for the management system project alongside other ongoing strategic projects in the organization. In this case it would be a great benefit for both representatives of top management and the strategic group to meet quite often at the beginning of the project in order to create both sustainable prerequisites and sponsorship for the work on the management system. A suggestion for project organization and participants when the management system project is on a large scale is as follows:

- *A project group* consisting of representatives for the operations, project manager, change management facilitator, and patient safety developer.
- *A project management team* giving directions to the project group. It benefits the project when having a formal sponsor. This team may include the CEO and the head of patient safety department.

- *A strategy group* providing the project group with aspirations to create excellence in future health care. This group can consist of management representatives, strategists and patient safety developers.
- *A workshop group* that creates major results for the project, such as process diagrams and the future management system structures. It would also outline the management system contents. Here are representatives from different professions and operations working to cover the whole process.

The project manager should be supported by the project sponsor when planning and organizing participants in the different groups, since the assigner has the mandate to grant participants time needed for the work. The project manager has the challenge and responsibility to draw up the time plan for different activities thoroughly as well as to make sure all the required conference rooms are available. Invitations to the seminars should be sent out well in advance. The same group members are also preferred. New members can slow down the working pace when they are obliged to catch up with all the new knowledge developed during the project especially when the rest of the group are fully versed.

Sometimes this is necessary with new group members and they need assistance with catching up, therefore documentation is of great importance. The size of the workshop group may vary depending on the size of the organization. It is central to cover all knowledge from all parts of the operations and from nearby operations. It is also vital to highlight some areas by inviting experts such as representatives from patient associations or external partners involved before and after the value chain. Such workshops may be performed in small groups and be reported further to the larger seminar group.

Working this way, it is easier to carry on delivering the project without slowing it down. Any delimitation should be well defined, creating a common picture of expectations within the group regarding what should and should not be done. Such clarity and consensus make prioritizing easier. Delimitations point out examples of what the management system should contain, who receives the management system content, whether it should be integrated with other management systems, and what effects are to be achieved.

Risks to the Project

Reorganizations are always a huge risk to any ongoing project, and such a profound project as designing or redesigning a management system is no exception. Reorganizations in management influence project work negatively when questioned or when the participants get limited possibilities to participate in and contribute to the project. Once again, the engagement in and understanding of the project value by top management is crucial to minimize disturbance. One way to reduce risks for the ongoing project is to run it on smaller scale. It is important to strive to achieve results step by step by making continuous progress in the work while showing useful outcomes.

Another risk is striving for perfection. High objectives, huge expectations, and bold ambitions create risk for creating too high a demand on quality and result. Then the perfectionism becomes an enemy of the good. The project may get caught in a search-for-ideal-structure loop and ambition to cover absolutely everything. When this happens, the management system may become a bureaucratic burden instead of a welcomed support. Be courageous and create subresults that are good enough or improved in comparison to the previous ones. Doing so will create room for development with options to complete subprojects and to improve one subproject after another while the overall project proceeds.

A further aspect while working on the management system project is taking a parallel look at the change-culture within the organization. Strong professional feelings and ego at different organizational levels may raise thick barriers for change to break through when communicating new insights and alternative solutions. Cooperation with change managers, if there are any, may help to understand current corporate challenges when managing change. Large projects demand a project manager who has profound knowledge about designing a sustainable management system, but I highly recommend also working with a highly skilled change management facilitator who runs the human side of change in parallel.

Communication Plan

Having clarified who is to attend the different seminars included in the project and who needs information, a simple communication plan can be created. When done, it is easier to stay in control of:

- Target groups for the information, for example, management
- Objectives of the information, for example, decisions on actions
- Planned activities, for example, who to invite to the different project meetings and workshops
- Decisions to be made, such as an expert's advice
- Schedules, for example, meeting every Wednesday nine am
- Individuals in charge of certain parts highlighted by using their initials
- Follow-ups, for example, where and when

The project should keep the communication plan up to date and well visible for all, not only those directly involved in the project. Using a whiteboard is an excellent choice and creates transparency, curiosity, and interest in the ongoing project.

Chart As-Is State

When all the initial decisions have been made, and the prerequisites have been clarified, the first part of the project may begin. It is about creating a common picture, within the project group, about the current state. This insight is necessary if you want to make sure to make informed decisions, instead of decisions based on unconfirmed assumptions. It is a demanding kind of detective work. The project group members must get clear insights into the problems and problem understanding in the organization. If there is a common understanding and the problems are well identified, then it will be easier for the project group to be supported when suggesting solutions. When the current situation is known and understood, the managers, based on this knowledge, can gain insights into what will be done and make relevant decisions.

In large organizations where management system projects tend to be large scale, it may be wise to run the project on two parallel tracks. The first track would run the management system project forward. The other track would run the human side of change of the project in order to work on the desired outcomes the management system should lead to, that is, changed behaviors. There are two different tasks: One is running the project and the other is supporting staff and managers to go along with the mental and cultural change required by the project. Many people are change-tired and resist change, thus well-planned change management is generally a good investment when answering a human's natural resistance to changes. Unanswered resistance to change is one of the most common reasons for project failure or to be less successful than expected (Hiatt 2006).

The next step is to decide where to start. The suggestion is to start where the project outcome is desired the most and where it creates most value in the shortest time. Once gaining results, the project's success ripples in the organization, and more and more staff will be willing to develop their part of the organization process. If the project is run top-down in the organizational hierarchy, omitting the cross-functional operational context, it may be perceived as an edict and contribute to building up a silent yet strong resistance and forming challenging informal leaders. This risk occurs when personnel are change-tired due to their executives' previous less successful attempts to manage change. The memories of projects where there was a lack of connection between decision and operational benefit are powerful (Hiatt 2006). But those memories can be transformed when change is managed professionally by creating space for trust, sharing and creating a common picture and understanding. Start by getting insights into the shortcomings with the existing management systems:

- What kinds of management systems already exist in the organization?
- How is the existing management system designed?
- What demands and objectives are fulfilled by the management system?

- Is the management system integrated to other management systems? If so, which ones?
- How updated is the existing management system?
- Is the management system easy to work with, for example, to maintain?
- Is the management system easy to use for users at the sharp end?
- Is the management system patient-process-oriented?
- Does the management system result in continuous operation improvements?
- Are there similar projects going on in the organization?
- How is the output monitored in the operation process?
- Where is the management system creating most value?
- Are there allocated resources aimed at maintaining and keeping the management system vivid?

Answering those questions gives valuable knowledge leading to insights into deficiencies and what needs to be done. The insights are going to be a foundation for the project group when presenting suggestions to managers on which decisions should be taken to be able to continue working on the management system project.

The next step is to look closer into the benefits and deficiencies in the existing management system. Look for good examples in your own organization first, and from other national and international perspectives. What does an existing best practice look like? What other successful possible ways are there to adopt? What has the latest research taught us? Try not to reinvent the wheel. Remember to look upstream and downstream in the value chains. When the first part of the project has been completed, gather all the project participants, project managers, and assigners together. Gather their expectations on the work and compare these to the collected results. Look at the results in a space of trust and cocreation. At this point, there is no room for showing off, but for sharing and creating common future objectives based on trust, teamwork, and knowledge.

Take the Next Step

Put together all the collected results so far and work out recommendations for how to proceed. Look at the expected outcomes of the management system and compare them to the "today-situation." The need for improvement can be visualized as a simple mathematical equation:

Expectations minus as-is situation = need for improvement

The need for improvement is in other words the same as the difference between expectations and the current state. Expectations are part of the prerequisites of the project and may be expressed as, for example, patient safety objectives, quality objectives, use of resources, or expenditure of time. Using the insights of current state as shown in the previous section helps to describe:

- The level of support existing management systems are able to provide today
- How well the organization is working according to existing management systems
- To what degree existing management systems are used today

Coming to this point the project manager and project members must decide what should be the next step. The project management should strive to use a "minimum effective dose" when making improvements, in order to get the most benefits from the least efforts possible. There are various possibilities for taking action as listed in Table 5.1.

Keep an eye on the scope because it is easy to make it too narrow. Make sure you are not creating patient risks later in the value chain downstream. Even though you have a feeling of being in control regarding patient safety in your own organization, risks may arise in the chain of different performers engaged in healthcare delivery. That is the main reason for a management system covering united actions with the world outside your organization.

Table 5.1 Management system project: As-is situation and proposals for action

As-is situation	Action proposal
We have sufficient management system, but patient safety is not provided for very well	Don't design a new management system, just for patient safety. Complete the current one instead of using mapped good examples and best practice. Make sure the implementation strategy is thoroughly thought out
Our management system is good enough and patient safety is well provided, but people are not using the management system	Verify whether the management system really gives a basis working toward expected objectives. You might find reasons for why it is not being used as expected. If the content is right, focus on creating better availability, user friendliness, and changing the management
We have a sufficient management system, but we don't know if it is in use	Have a closer look at the operations follow-ups. There needs to be a connection between a management system and follow-ups
We are doing a good job and providing good patient safety, but not according to the management system	Update the management system by mapping work as done. Update even roles and procedure descriptions. Engage personnel in change management, making sure the management system contributes to creation of learning organization
We are not using our management system very much. We complete it with separate papers, notes, and prints. We belive that we provide good patient safety	There are many reasons to create standardized workflows, described in an updated management system. New procedures for operational follow-ups are required and there is a great need for change management work as well. The staff are probably working on their own and in different ways. It will take some time and hard work to create common procedures mirroring daily work. It is important not to impose changes but to make use of all good work solutions worked out for a long time
We underperform and we must improve patient safety dramatically and we need to design a management system	Make sure the project continues mapping today's processes and create suggestions for new ones. Make sure these stand up to expectations. New processes create changes, and changes take resources and time. For this reason, try to find the "minimum effective dose" starting with pilot activities. When working by the desk think wide, big, and in long- term strategy. When trying out new processes, do it in small steps. It helps getting ahead starting with small changes, but making big effects

So far, the following should be in place:

- A powerful and engaged assigner.
- An engaged and well-informed management group.
- Project benefits well known in the organization.
- Identified and reviewed management system deficiencies.
- Suggestions for project continuation developing both management systems and operations.
- Everyone involved in the project organization understands to what degree the rest of the organization is aware of existing shortcomings with existing management systems, and a plan has been made for managing this awareness.
- Members of project organization have been chosen, invited to all workshops, and have assured their participation.
- Old and current management systems are known. Ongoing parallel projects are known as well.

Knowledge concerning current situations and all the insights from a basis and starting point need to have been collected when choosing actions required for moving the project ahead. When you have come this far, it's time to decide the structure of the management system for patient-safe care.

Design To-Be Management System Structure

When designing the management system structure, keep in mind the fact that the personnel at the sharp end play the critical role when delivering patient-safe care, having local knowledge, an ability to adapt and know-how, which is necessary to make the work done on a daily basis in a continually changing context. A common issue is where to put information or documents in a database.

A common trap is to put the document where it fits within the system, without thinking "how someone is going to find this information." This "someone" may be a new employee with good professional knowledge but has not yet learned the specifics of the new workplace, for example, where things are stored, how to contact on duty medics, or how to report an adverse event. When this basic kind of information is hard to find, people easily become dependent on asking colleagues questions. These kinds of questions can also affect experienced personnel when a rare event occurs. Then the need of a reminder about how to do things arises. A well-designed management system will in such cases function as a support to daily work. If the design is poor, it is going to be easier to ask a workmate a question than search it on the system. People will learn quickly not to trust and not to use the management system. Instead they will discuss their problems and do as they usually do, in the worst case following old instructions from a binder, without knowing when the last update was done. Moreover, it is disturbing to be interrupted while, for example, writing a prescription, giving an injection, or calculating drug dosage, and takes time from patient-care-time or other value-creating work. Then the vicious circle pictured in figure 5.1 is a fact. The good circle is to prefer because easy to find and correct information results in more time for delivering care, less stress for personnel, and thereby increased patient safety.

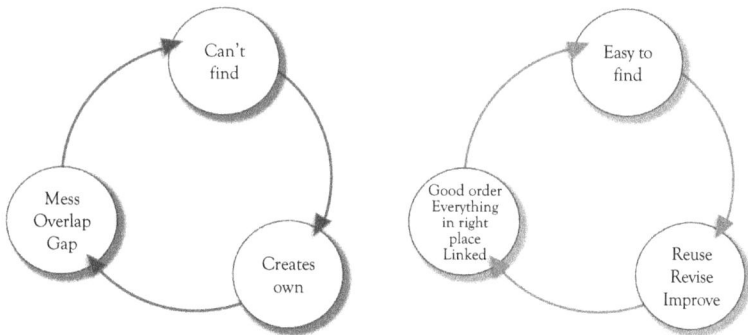

Figure 5.1 The vicious circle and the good circle

The structure of the management system is the sequence by which the content is sorted, like a table of contents. There are two ways of looking at the structure of a management system. You can choose to see it as:

1. A structure for an effective way to put in information to the management system, or
2. A structure for finding and using information for users needing it in order to perform their tasks safely and efficiently

Many management systems are designed for effective ways to put in information. Then everything is arranged in order to be easily maintained. This outlook helps keep the management system up to date and follows the logic of its creator and is easy to work with. Unfortunately, it doesn't automatically mean that the structure is user-friendly. An alternative outlook, which I am describing in this book, is focused on designing an easy-to-find information structure. There are many more users searching for information in the management system, than those who are entering information onto the system. Nevertheless, the structure is, unfortunately, seldom designed for the needs of the users at the sharp end.

Now, you have a chance to change that by exploring how to design a structure that meets both needs: to easily find things and easily maintain them. There are intelligent computer software products, such as Qualiware and QPR[1] that support organizing the content of management systems. These software products often have a hidden structure that is visible only to those who maintain and manage the management system. On top of this hidden structure, such software enables several usage structures, customized to different target groups. Here we address how the maintenance structure looks, that is, the management system structure which is used to logically place the right thing in the right place, regardless of how it is exposed for a user.

Finding structure for management system may be difficult; therefore it is useful to comply with a few principles, when working out the structure. Following these principles will help you to create a structure that is going to be:

- Consistent
- Easy to recognize
- Robust to organizational changes

Let me highlight the constructing mindset by using a silly Swedish song[2] that tells a story about a boy who went to school and learned how

---

[1] https://qualiware.com and https://qpr.com
[2] Karl Nilsson by Povel Ramel

to spell, how to read, how to write, how to count, and physics. We can recognize five knowledge categories in the lyrics: spelling, reading, writing, counting, and physics. As you may have noticed, physics is deviant in this classification because the others are know-how subjects, while physics is a subject field where you use know-hows. Unfortunately, many management systems structures are not consistent when categorizing information and consequently make the system hard to use.

A well-designed management system categorizes its "software," that is, knowledge, written down in an easy-to-use and easy-to-maintain way. In other words, the management system structure should separate spelling, reading, writing, and counting, from physics. A structure with consistent categorization is necessary when creating easy-to-find content, not only for the creator of the structure but, above all, for those who work at the sharp end, with the information.

The further the distance from the blunt end of the management creation system to the reality of users at the sharp end, the bigger risk there is for creating descriptions from an imaginary world. These are hard to follow and encourage dangerous work around. I wish to give prominence to the importance of designing the structure considering the needs of users. In the following section you will get some ideas on how to create such a structure.

Principles for Creating a Management System Structure

Following a set of principles, described as follows, will protect consistency and usability of the management system content. Regard the structure as a multidimensional tree with more and more fine branches. The stems and the main branches answer to the levels of the management system. Each time a stem branches the management system, the user must understand how it branches, what can be expected when following a certain branch by understanding how they divide. As the branches become finer in this tree ending with the leaves, more precise information is found in the structure.

The principle of type-safe structure is as follows: Whenever a stem is divided into branches, these branches must be:

- Exhaustive
- Named clearly to distinguish between the branches and
- Divided using the same criterion; they share the same categorization discriminator

When a categorization of something is "type-safe", anything can fit into one type without having a type called "others." A simple type-safe categorization would for instance be:

- Up to 18-year-olds are referred to as "kids."
- Over 18 but under 70 years are referred to as "grown-ups."
- Over 70-year-olds are referred as "old people."

This categorization is truly type-safe as it is exhaustive, and it is obvious where to place or find information for any occasion, and a person's age is used as a category discriminator.

Let us go back to the silly song in the previous section. It was about a boy who learned to *spell,* to *read,* to *write,* to *count,* and *physics.* Spelling, reading, and counting are types of knowledge while physics is a subject field. This is not a type-safe categorization of knowledge. But it is a good example of how many management systems unfortunately are structured; when branching information, the discriminator is unclear, or even missing, and the categories are not exhaustive. If the boy wanted to read a book about how to calculate particle movements, it would fit into the "read," "calculate," and "physics" categories. This vicious circle pictured in Figure 5.1 will spin faster and faster as such structures grow; picture five people who make updates in such structures over a long period of time. They would use type-unsafe structures differently making it hard to find information in it and hard to maintain.

Type-safe categorization of information is something to aim at, as far as practically possible, but it is very hard to accomplish completely. It takes practice to get the type-safe feeling for classification and categorization knowledge. You will need to exercise patience, do consequent thinking, and gain in experience. The reward will appear as good user-friendliness.

In the following text you can see examples of three classifications that use separate discriminators: subject or specialty, steps in processes, and supportive functions.

- Subject/specialty, such as
  Cardiology
  Orthopedy
  Oncology
  Nursing
  Physiotherapy
- Steps in core processes, such as
  Collecting anamnesis
  Blood test analysis
  Delivering treatment
- Grouping the supportive functions, such as
  HR
  Cleaning, food supply
  IT

Note that the examples above are not exhaustive.

Consequently, within the "Specialty" class there should only be specialties honoring the principle of keeping just one discriminatory ground rule within a class. An underlying level to the "Specialty" class can, however, have another discriminator; for example, under *Cardiology* you might find a level containing the process steps (and only process steps) where new process steps or activity descriptions may be placed. Figure 5.2 shows an example of classifications in three levels, where each level is having its own discrimination rule. It is important to remember that the principle for the discriminator must be consistent at every level. Then the structure is "type-safe," clear, and an exhaustive classification using the same discrimination rule.

Cardiology
Admit patient
>   Check patient's identity
>   Have a patient-nurse conversation
>   Decide on inquiry
Inquire
>   Obtain the anamnesis
>   Take blood tests
>   ECG
>   Perform an ultrasound examination
>   Perform an angiography
>   Decide on the next step
Take actions and give treatment
>   Insert stent
>   Insert pacemaker
>   Perform cardiac by-pass surgery
Make a follow-up appointment

Orthopedy
Admit patient
>   Check patient's identity
>   Have a patient-nurse conversation
>   Decide on inquiry
Inquire
>   Obtain the anamnesis
>   Prepare patient for surgery
>   ...
>   ...

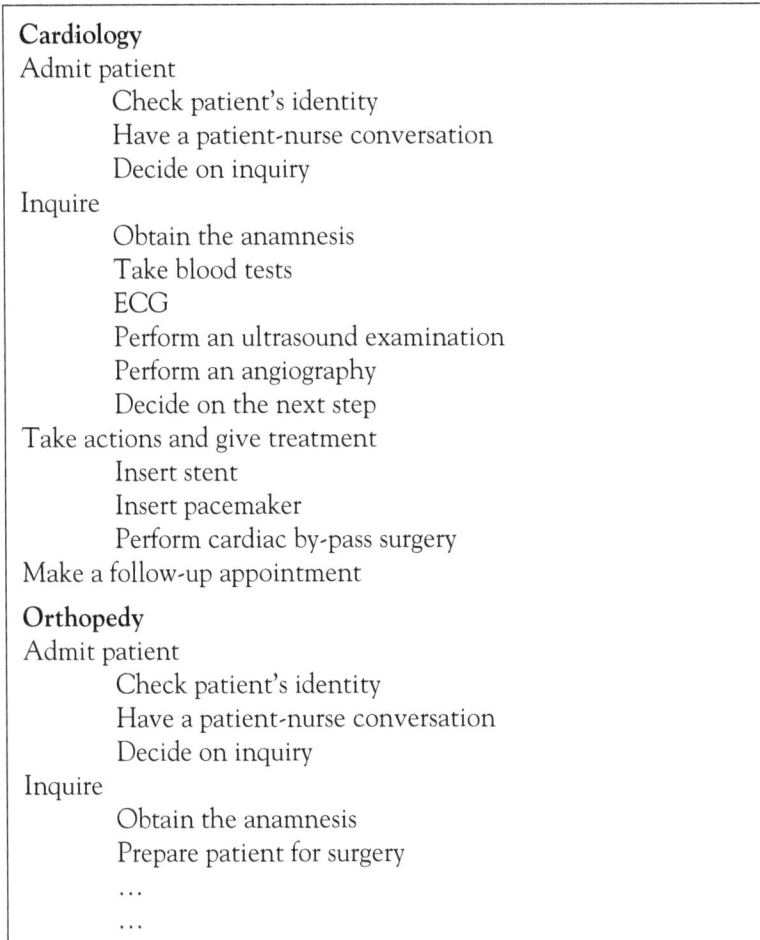

Figure 5.2 Example of classifications in three levels, each level having its own discrimination rule

Note that the examples in Figure 5.2 are not exhaustive. The earlier example divides the process "*Admit patient*" into activities together with the patient. The idea is that every step is to be done. The "*Inquiry*" is also divided into activities and is placed in some order between the steps. The last one "Take actions and give treatment" has a different discriminator. In this case you don't have a series of activities arranged in a process. Instead there are different treatment alternatives to choose from although the structure is created in the same way. A type-safe structure is much more sustainable over time if it is designed in the right way.

Then the system's discriminators have long life cycles and demand less time to be maintained. Below you will find some ideas on how to find durable structures and others which do not.

Durable structure:

- *Subject/specialty*, for example, cardiology, orthopedy, oncology, anesthetic nursing. Subject fields tend to last long. These may have their own place in the management system. Be aware of the fact that different subject fields contain parts of common knowledge. For example, procedure description for how to deal with anaphylaxis or giving CPR should be the same in all units of a hospital or even in a country as a whole, following national guidelines. The procedure for how to deal with low plasma-glucose levels should also be the same regardless of care given in the emergency unit, outpatient surgery unit, or the ward specialized in diabetes. On the other hand, general knowledge for all the fields may be placed under separate captions using another discriminator. For example, procedures for taking blood tests, handling cytostatics, diluting drugs diagrams, reporting using MEWS (modified early warning scale), handling suspect sepsis, or following basic hygiene rules, all these or the like may be placed under general captions. These descriptions should be formulated and kept up to date by a specialist who knows the professional know-how in order to avoid dangerous reality gaps between work as done and work as imagined. The idea is about spreading and reusing common knowledge and the best practice wherever possible, and at the same time to avoid local variations.

- *Processes names* on an overall level, for example, admitting patient, inquiring, giving treatment. When the process becomes more detailed, the variations appear.

- *Places and bigger items.* Bigger constructions like radiation therapy machines are rarely to be moved. That is the reason to use these as a hanger for information. For example, user manuals can be found under caption *Equipment* rather than under the processes where the equipment is used.

Less durable structure:

- *Organizational structure.* The organizational structure may sometimes coincide with some of the durable examples shown previously, but you should notice the difference between a durable subject categorization and an organizational unit. There may be several orthopedic receptions (= organizational units) which may very well share the same management system.

- *Who does what in a process.* Write down the role but not the position in process descriptions. Positions may be changed due to reorganizations, while the roles, for example, surgeon, nurse, or therapist, usually remain.

- Try to avoid writing down *names* and *phone numbers* in the instructions.

To sum up, it is good practice to separate information that often changes from more solid information. For this reason, write down more temporary information and more permanent information in two separate documents. Otherwise the management system will be hard to keep updated due to upcoming changes and increasing contradictions. For example, it is preferable to differ between role descriptions and role owner from staff names in the descriptions.

If there aren't any clear processes, that is, a natural series of steps to be done, then I recommend categorizing the procedures in *planned, unplanned,* and *urgent.*

- Planned/prophylactic: Work is done by procedure, it is done automatically "with the spine," it is "every body's" job, the way it is usually done.

- Unplanned/putting things right: Directed by the occurring events, infrequent events.

- Urgent: When it emerges, you need to find the correct information quickly and easily.

There may be a near infinite number of unplanned or urgent events. However, the care givers' capabilities to meet these events are not infinite. For instance, the capability to perform a CT scan on a trauma patient in an emergency situation is quite similar to performing a scheduled scan on a multimorbid patient. These events may share procedure descriptions.

Preferably, create a flat and shallow structure rather than one with many deep and narrow levels. It will be easier to honor the classification principles mentioned above, and, it will take less time for the user to find the required information. A broader structure provides its users with an overview and a wider range of alternatives when searching.

A deep structure encourages creating unnatural levels and tags which can be difficult to understand, in particular for nonspecialists. One way to scrutinize the structure usability is to see how easy it is for new employees to use the management system, such as professionals who need to find information in an organization that is new to them. Another scenario for testing the structure is to let existing staff find procedures for events that rarely occur.

Workflow When Designing Management System Structure

Finding structure for a management system may be challenging. A good way to start work is to ask the project group: "What content is of interest to bring into the management system?" Write the answers down and capture all the words that reflect the future content of the management system. Thus, I suggest you gather all the members of the project and work as follows. Book a conference room with big whiteboard and prepare post-it notes and pencils. Notes are very useful since you can easily change their place on the white board. It is usual to use 30 to 50 notes. Check against the current management system in order to find as exhaustive a structure as possible. Before the workshop, you may prepare the notes with headings, as shown in Table 5.2.

Table 5.2 Workflow when creating structure for management system

Dimension	Explanation	Content examples
What, subject	Equipment, for example, dialyzer, MRI	Instructions and safety regulations for handling, qualifications, and maintaining regulations
What, subject field	Specialization, for example, cardiology, oncology, imaging, nursing	Processes and routine descriptions within specialties. Read more in the following text
Where, places	From the hospital area map, to a single supply cabinet	Instructions for how to refill supply depot
How, next to the patient	Process chain, following the patient, or supporting work close to the patient. Step-by-step description of how the work is done IRL	Admit patient, have conversation with patient Read more in the following text
How, generally	Processes and activities, descriptions of how something gets done	Purchasing supplies, recruiting personnel, managing waste disposal. Read more in the following text
Who, internally	Roles, organization structure	Descriptions of functions, delegation, competences, and qualifications
Who, externally	Stakeholders, cooperations	Agreements with care center, transportation, meal supplier
Why	Objectives and follow-ups	Objectives, indicators, and measurement. How measurement and reporting are to be done

Please notice that these dimensions do not make up the structure, but they are very helpful in finding it. By preparing the captions shown in Table 5.2 the team members will find it easier to write down the words on the notes. If you can place the notes within the dimensions, then the word describing the content is useful when designing the structure. Don't be afraid of experimenting with the structure moving the notes up and down to different levels, for example, processes within cardiology, purchase, or links to how to connect things. Try different process titles when naming. Words like patient safety are usually preferable to work into some of the divisions. Thus, instead of creating a division on its own level in the structure hierarchy, let patient safety show up in different contexts further down in the structure. Check out if the existing management system fits in. Is there a natural place for a certain instruction? If some information or instruction fits in to more than one place, then consider placing it where it is needed. You may also divide the instruction into two overlapping instructions and refer these to each other. From the maintenance point of view there is always a risk of having overlapping instructions or placing them in several places.

Make sure you retain the width of the process perspective and the end-to-end value chains they take part in. The scope should be wide enough to cover the patient's whole journey: from arisen need until the need is cared for or has ceased. You don't need to cover the whole context though. For example, the processes should have demarcations broader than your own organization, but it is enough to describe your own function roles. The main point is to cover the organizations' interface relations and dependencies and not just the internal ones. If you want to be very ambitious and create a super robust management system structure, then information modeling can be a way. Information modeling is a categorization technique that strictly looks at the information flow, neutral from organization, processes, geography, or IT-systems. The result is an information model that helps to define the structure and content of the management system. Finally, it is a great support when formulating demands on the future IT-system for storage of the management system.

Describe and Improve Processes

Earlier, you learned about basic process knowledge and practical hints for drawing processes in a durable way. Working on process descriptions demands time, endurance, and reflection, thus it should be done in a quiet environment free from phone calls or staff locators. Work in a room with a big whiteboard so everybody in the seminar group can clearly see the progress in work. Process mapping work is demanding but it is easy to believe it is a simple task when you see a process that is both easy to follow and to understand. As a matter of fact, process modeling is a profession[3] on its own; therefore I usually recommend hiring a facilitator who is an

---

[3] https://pdfs.semanticscholar.org/404d/bbe924d63fe6089fad-83b4e888143c391015.pdf

experienced modeler and neutral to the organization. If there is a need for reorganization and many changes must be made, it is easier for a neutral outsider to evaluate the as-is situation and help the organization forward. It is most likely you will have to meet several times to work on the process mapping, since different process outcomes are going to show up. Processes can be described from different outlooks and levels.

- A process map with a value chain drawn from the perspective of the patient and his/her relatives, the so-called end-to-end processes. These kinds of processes start where the need has arisen and continue all the way, until the need is satisfied or has ceased.
- A high-level process map showing how different parties, authorities, and organizations cooperate.
- Detailed processes representing *work as done* on a daily basis.

Moreover, process descriptions can be made from the perspective of the as-is situation or the desired to-be situation. The as-is outlook would describe the current workflow and the to-be outlook would describe desired workflow. Let the needs of your organization decide which outlook is best to choose, assuming high patient safety is always in focus. Write down the content of the process-fish graphics on big post-it notes. It is convenient to be able to rearrange the notes using the whiteboard and making it easy for all participants to interact with the work.

- While working, focus on the time sequence the activities are done within, instead of organizational boundaries and functions.
- Describe exactly what the process *looks like* and focus on what is going on.
- Avoid the temptation to describe it as it should be, or how the work is done and by whom.
- Take pictures of the process map for documentation and save these during the whole mapping process.
- Make sure the project group members agree on the descriptions picturing *work as done*.

- Remember to stretch out the process a couple of steps outside your organization. It may be a good idea to invite representatives from adjoining operations. Shared knowledge about what happens upstream and downstream of the process precludes misunderstandings and dangerous information gaps where many adverse events occur.

It is very natural when working on process mapping to discover steps missing in the description. The steps are often so obvious they are forgotten at the beginning. Fortunately working with post-it notes makes it easy to make room in the activity chain for the forgotten ones. As I mentioned in the chapter about basic process knowledge, there is a wide range of benefits using process documentation. Regardless of the reason for doing the work the documentation should always be clear and easy to understand. In particular when working on a management system, the process documentation should comply with the following:

- Process maps should be "dense," meaning free from gaps, especially when accountabilities are handled further on between parties, for example, different care suppliers or different units.
- Process maps aiming to function as a base for a management system structure should follow the principles of a management system structure, as mentioned in an earlier section.
- Activity diagrams describe work as done, expressed in a way all personnel at the sharp end can recognize and use as support on a daily basis. It may even be used, for example, as support when introducing new employees to the workplace.
- Alternative outcomes from important activities or even processes are well covered, guiding how to handle predictable and different possible outcomes.

There is a big difference between *process description* and *process improvement.* The first is about illustrating and documenting operations using the process outlook. Working on a management system means to refresh the documentation making *work as done* illustrated. The second one, *improving* processes, is about developing operations aimed at improving workflows, increased patient safety, higher quality, and lower costs. As for the management system project, this would bring a very different assignment. If you choose to improve the processes as well, you'll need to extend the project workflow.

- Use the need for improvement as a starting point and use results from the as-is situation mapping. Go back to the expressed expectations and reflect on what is needed to fulfill these. It may be about missing knowledge, bad timing, or insufficient information availability.
- Describe today's processes, just well enough to cover and understand the extended range of the process without getting into details.
- Study the as-is process trying to understand what is needed to meet the expectations. Ask yourself if there are any barriers, when and where deficits may arise. Observe these as symptoms and not as a cause. Obstacles occurring in processes usually start in previous processes.
- Study good examples and solutions used in other places thoroughly. Be brave and look beyond your boundaries of organization and knowledge.
- Design different process suggestions and try these ideas to see whether they can meet the challenge, but the ideas can't be vague. The project group delivering the development proposition needs to make calculations and simulations to be able to see improvement effects, for example, saving time, lowering costs, and improving quality, proving the change will bring real improvements. If the changes are small, calculating in Excel® may be enough. For the big ones you may need help using a decision simulation tool, for example, World Modeler®. Strive for simple solutions using "the lowest effective dose" for desired outcome. Make representatives from the steering committee involved in simulation work aiming to

get support in the hierarchy as soon as possible, in order to develop implementation plans.

- Create suggestions for the implementation plan. If the process changes are to be a success, they should be implemented one at the time in pilot projects.

Now let's take the next creating step, which is filling the management system with content.

Fill the Management System With Content

Now you have come this far, it is time to fill the management system with content and the following should be available:

- A structure divided in levels
- A process map partly useful as a structure for the management system
- Activity models showing how the work is done in real life regarding processes *not in need* of improvement
- Activity models showing how the work should be done (agreed and desired), regarding the processes *in need* of improvement
- Procedure descriptions and instructions from existing management systems, reviewed as useful in the new management system and possibly to be reused

Having come so far you have another big task to accomplish, namely to compose a new management system content and rewrite the old one. Now it is also time to engage experts from different subject fields to join the work. You will not be able to just copy their texts because they usually are not familiar with the principles for management systems in the way project members are. In order to be sure that all the content is of the same quality, both the new texts and the old ones from the current management system must be reviewed. The next section presents some more principles which are important to follow and honor.

Principles for Designing Management System Content

Using basic principles to support you when designing content makes your work easier. As mentioned before, the management system structure is a kind of index, which resembles a tree trunk and branches. The content, that is, all the information such as the text, pictures, and other descriptions, is similar to the leaves in the tree structure. The content should be designed according to the following principles:

1. **Describe one thing at a time.**
2. **Connect the description to the lifecycle of the subject being described.**
3. **Make descriptions short.**
4. **Describe the work as done.**

These content principles are valid regardless of storing the content in a database or visible text on the intranet.

1. Describe one thing at a time

means that it is *one* work effort, *one* activity, or *one* material described and that descriptions are *not* mixed together with another description. For example, instruction for how to measure patients' blood pressure:

- Choose the right arm (except if the arm is paralyzed, has lymphatic edema or dialysis fistula).
- Choose the correct sphygmomanometer size.

This description includes only the description of how to measure blood pressure, because that is just what the heading says. Do not fall into the temptation and write down how to calibrate the sphygmomanometer because it doesn't belong to this how-to-do knowledge. Keeping these apart makes it easier to find the desired information and to find the right heading.

2. Connecting the description to the lifecycle of the subject being described.

The description of how to measure blood pressure is valid as long as experts consider this is the right way of doing it. If the description included storage place and instructions for calibration of the instrument, there would be a risk of decreased actuality of the content arising. The procedure is the same even if the storage place is changed or if new blood pressure monitors were used. Place, role, object, and procedure, all these have different life cycles. Therefore, the description of a subject in the management system should be connected to the life cycle of the subject being described. In the long run it is preferable to keep procedure, object, place, and roles apart. Add cross-references from procedure description to instrument storage description, and from instrument storage description to calibration/maintenance description. Then you can make changes in the actual text. It also makes it easier to reuse information. Looking at the blood pressure example, procedure *Measure blood pressure using sphygmomanometer and stethoscope* would be valid regardless of the unit in a hospital, health center, or reception. Other examples where procedures could be reused in the whole organization are dealing with a calicivirus outbreak, giving CPR, handling suspect anaphylaxis, handling suspect sepsis, and many, many more.

3. **Short descriptions or paragraphs.**

It is easy to fall into temptation and try to cover all the aspects in one document, producing a huge amount of text to be read in order to find relevant information. Carthey et al. (2011) suggest when writing or reviewing policies or guidelines to consider whether volume, version control, accessibility, length, or titling problems may increase the risk of noncompliance. The management systems are filled with many pages of long instructions which few people have enough time to read because there is too much information. As always there are pros and cons, so it is important to find a balance between how detailed the descriptions are and how many cross-references are added. When the management system is based on short texts in several small documents, it will be more complex because of the many references, but there are advantages.

- It works well for information with a short life cycle that needs to be adjusted more often, and of interest to many people.

- It is easy to keep information updated since you need to rewrite just in one place.
- Reusing information is made easier, which is perfect for spreading good practice and newfound knowledge.

The disadvantages are:
- Higher costs due to having more reference documents to update.
- The user will have to search for several documents to get the whole picture.

One way to solve the problem is to place the same information in different places in the management system structure. For example, instead of referring to another document placed in a different part of the management system about calibration of the sphygmomanometer, you can put document copies where they may be needed. The opposite scenario would be fewer and bigger documents. Advantages and disadvantages will of course be the opposite. Documents become more complicated and with broader content. There will be more overlapping of information and more areas to keep updated. Bigger documents, however, work well when containing information with a long life cycle.

4. Describing work as done.

Fill the management system with content describing work done when it goes right, instead of descriptions of how to avoid known errors. This approach results in a dynamic management system filled with good examples, best practice. and shared knowledge. If healthcare professionals can see the need for a policy, procedure description, or guideline, and if it is written in a way that shows a practical understanding of the real world, and finally, if it is easy to access and follow, staff are more likely to comply with the document (Carthey et al. 2011). Management systems typically contain descriptions about how to avoid errors. The content is often an overload of root-cause investigations, adverse event reports, and discovered risks, all in compliance with the Safety-I outlook.

Reactive organization	Conscious organization	Promoting organization
• Acts on what went wrong • Analyzes events • Monitors aberrations • Searches for faults systematically • Focus on failed performance	• Acts on what went wrong • Analyzes events • Works on prevention of harm • Identifies risks using simple risk-assessment methods • Main focus on failed performance	• Strengthen successful actions • Works proactively • Monitor what went right • Focus on successful ways of work • Uses complex risk assessment methods • Fulfills legal demands • Fulfills patient´s expectations • Learning organization
Most expensive organization	Next most expensive organization	Economy in balance

SAFETY I ⟵   ⟶ SAFETY II

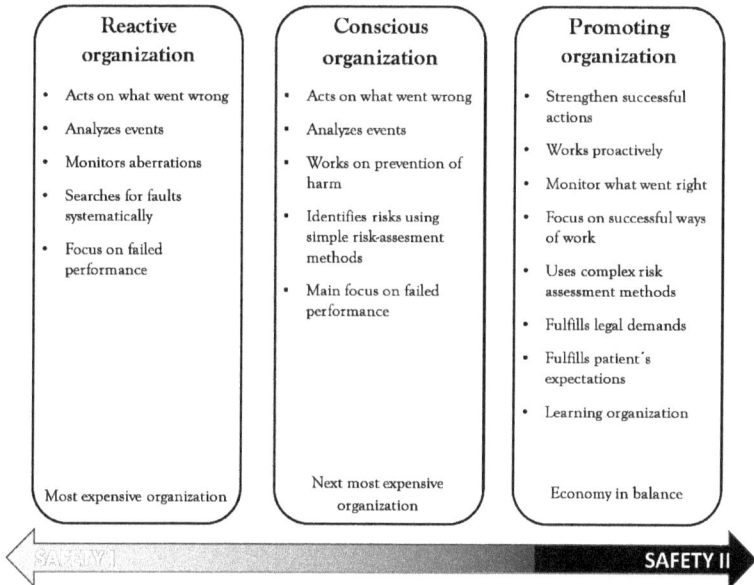

Figure 5.3 Maturity of management system for patient-safe care

Figure 5.3 illustrates three different outlooks of the management system. The first one is reactive to errors, the second one is mixed, and the
third one promotes a learning organization and improvement culture,
based on Safety-II. The way safety management is implemented into
the management systems mirrors organizations' outlook on safety and
thereby shows the way safety issues should be managed.

Describe Activities

Detailed descriptions of how the work is done must be placed somewhere
in the management system. The best place to store this information is in
the descriptions of process activities. That is the reason why you should go
back to process maps and activity diagrams made earlier when filling the
management system with content. Activity descriptions will then become
a natural place to search for relevant information and also easy to find.
Just to be well defined, in this context, I use the term activity description
instead of procedure description. Activity is always a part of a process at
its lowest level, which lies in process definition. The word *procedure* has
a broader use and sometimes refers to a process and sometimes to an
activity and is why I avoid it in this paragraph. It is quite usual for process

maps and activity diagrams to be changed, when they are about to be connected to their descriptions. The headings are to be changed, activities are merged or divided, and the process boundaries are moved. This is a natural process when details are to be set. Just make sure the changes are consistent throughout the entire process material as they may affect the entire content. A complete activity description contains the following:

- *A unique activity ID.* It makes it possible to reuse activity description. The same kind of activity may show up in a different process and it is useful to reuse the information. The activity ID should be a neutral serial number. Avoid serial numbers connected to the organization because these easily become outdated due to reorganizations.
- *An activity name.* Name the activity according to rules for name giving process.
- *Criterion for activity to start and for the starting event.*
- *The purpose of the activity.* This is to avoid gaps between activities and it also gives an explanation about why this should be done.
- *The activity results.* The distinct result of the activity and the receiver of this result. The result should fulfill the aim of activity.
- *A description.* The text describing how the work is done. Written in detailed steps, concisely, and in the imperative.
- *The role which mostly performs the activity.* Never write people's names here. The roles remain and people move around.
- *Other participants contributing or influencing.* Mention other parties who participate or are stakeholders. When more than one person is involved in an activity, it may help to clarify who has the main responsibility and what roles the others involved have.
- *The equipment.* What kind of equipment or consumable materials are required.
- *The checklist.* Keep it simple with bullet points and key words.
- *The author of description and the date when description was made.* It should always be attached, as it is important to con-

firm actuality of the content. Here it may be a good idea to place the author's name and role in case there are suggestions for changes and improvement occurs.

There is no need to describe all the characteristics mentioned previously in the complete activity description. For example, there will not always be several steps in an activity, or there is no need for material, or just one person does it. It may also be the case when the activity is obviously a part of basic knowledge connected to a registered profession and requires no further explanation. The rule of thumb is *describe as much as necessary*, no more.

An extensive documentation is not automatically better. In some cases, the only description for an activity is a checklist provided with ID, the purpose, the date, and who wrote it down. My final advice is to be thorough when you describe new or heavily changed activities.

Handle Variations

The daily work in healthcare and care settings is filled with variations, and high exceptions are common. Some variations are predictable, but many are not. The Safety-II approach teaches us that variability and personnel's ability to adjust according to variations make work done on a daily basis and can neither be described nor be foreseen in every detail. Still some variations in outcomes are predictable and easier to deal with when personnel know how to handle the alternative outcomes. For example, the usual outcome from an activity *Check health status and patient's own preparations* (just before surgery) in the activity diagram shown in Figure 5.4 is hopefully a patient ready for surgery. The patient has also followed instructions, for example, about fasting, presurgery shower, and medication. Now imagine that during the presurgery conversation some new facts are discovered, and unplanned activities must be done, for example, blood test due to anticoagulant medication or diabetes. As a result, the surgery schedule must be redone. Figure 5.4 show how this kind of alternative activity may be pictured in the activity diagram.

```
Patient        Check                          Check
arrived at     patient's      Admit the    health staus      OK      Check
the hospital   identity       patient          and                 parameters
                                            patient's
                                               own
                                           preparations

              Hospital       RN at operation  RN at operation      RN at operation
              reception      theatre          theatre              theatre


                                              Need of new
                                              blood tests
                                                              Take new
                                                              blood tests


                                                         RN at
                                                         outpatient
                                                         surgery unit
```

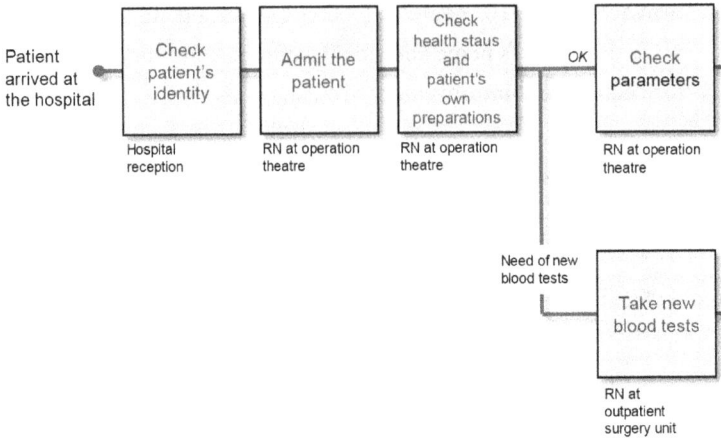

Figure 5.4 Activity diagram, a part of check health status and patient's own preparation process

It is important to create a space in the management system for such variations for two reasons. First, it is less stressful for personnel when knowing how to deal with it. Second, when bringing to awareness what could happen, everybody gets a chance to prevent variations causing a waste of resources, time waste, and troubling patients.

When you want to understand the context of a process and the dependencies between activities then I recommend completing the process map using the FRAM (Functional Resonance Analysis Method) found and described by professor Hollnagel (2012). The approach of FRAM is based on the comprehension of personnel working at the sharp end who are the best to know how the system functions and how the work should be done. They are also the best to know the variety of daily work and how to deal with it. A FRAM model helps to see the variations and the many couplings and dependencies, connecting activities together. Analyzing the result gives a broader understanding of how different outcomes may emerge and suggests alternative ways to organize the daily workflow. The method works very well when, for example, working on risk assessment or doing adverse event investigation.

Give Name to Headings and Content

Keeping both the documentation and naming updated helps to find information in the system, and it is far-reaching and important work.

In most workplaces there are a vast number of documents. Quite often the headings start with word "procedure" or "policy." Beginning the heading with this kind of word underlines the status of the document and explains very little of what it is about. Moreover, it makes it difficult to manage. Another common mistake is a heading that doesn't explain the context or when the content is useful. For example, *Give information to patient* doesn't tell the reader anything about what information is to be given. Is it prior to surgery? Is the information about medication compliance or perhaps the adverse effects of radiation therapy? It is possible to bring more clarity by following simple name giving—standard—principles. It is also about using the same principles when naming something: at every step, procedure, and object, and doing it consequently at all levels in the management system. The principles are listed as follows:

- *Standardize naming.* Utilities, for example, compress or a peripheral venous catheter (PVC), regardless of brand. Write *enroll* in other words *what*, and then clarify by adding *who*, *what*, or *when*, for example, child, another language, easy to understand English, prior to anesthesia.
- *Always write verb and subject in the heading.* It is not enough to write *Schedule* as heading or process name. The reader then has no clue what is about to be scheduled.
- *Define.* For example, what a PVC is, and agree on using one naming instead of three: PVC, PVL, and PVA. If, for example, you are using a surgical planning tool, use the same terminology and use the same standardized content in the whole organization. Abbreviations should be explained and standardized. Collect all agreed terms in a glossary and make sure it is consequently used in the management system. The glossary will become in itself a valuable part of the management system.
- *Define important general management system conceptions.* Used in the management system, for example, management, system, leadership, safety, patient safety, quality, procedure, process.

- *Establish an abbreviation glossary.* Don't assume everybody understands all the abbreviations used in a workplace. Create clarity and be generous in helping to avoid misunderstandings.
- *Establish organizational glossary* containing unit names and other close parties.
- *Establish role list.*

The staff working on these structures should be wearing "outsider lenses." A source of understanding what needs more clarification is to talk to new employees or stand-ins. They will quickly discover which abbreviations or synonyms need to be explained in descriptions, procedures, or information on the intranet. The ordinary personnel are often used to small infirmities in headings and texts and think they know how it should be. This can lead to risks and misunderstandings. Besides even experienced personnel are in need of structure, help, and support.

Connect Documents to Processes

The management system will contain many widely different kinds of documents and descriptions, from detailed manuals for advanced equipment to overall guidelines. The principles suggested in the previous paragraphs recommend that the management system is most durable and user-friendly when descriptions are placed in the right place of the structure and when the content of documents is not mixed. The next step is to connect the information to processes and activities. Visualize the management system structure, following process structure (see example in chapter 4, processes in different levels) like an index or a menu on the intranet. High-level processes are placed in the highest position of the structure. Logically, more overall descriptions should be connected to those, for example, guidelines, overall objectives, policies, requirements, instructions, and assignments applying to general underlying processes.

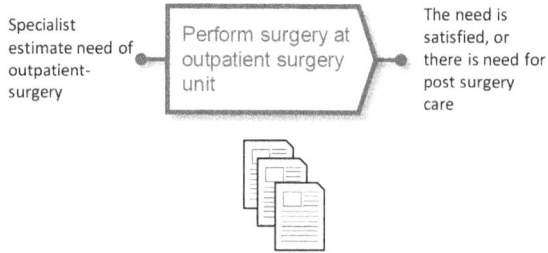

Figure 5.5 *Documents in the management system connected to the process*

To more detailed activity descriptions, it is preferable to connect documents describing work in steps, checklists, and so on as shown in Figure 5.5. This makes it easier to find required information when those descriptions are delimitated describing just one activity. Not all activities are to be connected to documents. Some are more general and placed higher up in the management system structure. Figure 5.6 gives an idea on how documents in the management system may be connected to single activities.

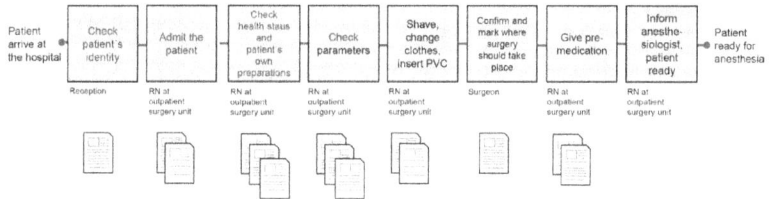

Figure 5.6 *Documents in the management system connected to single activities*

To sum up, it is convenient and possible to connect several different documents to a single activity. Moreover, an activity may be the usage of advanced equipment and therefore contains a reference to the user manual, or a certain part of the manual. It may be about patient pamphlets, document templates, or links to relevant drug information. It might be useful information just for a specific activity, as shown in Figure 5.7.

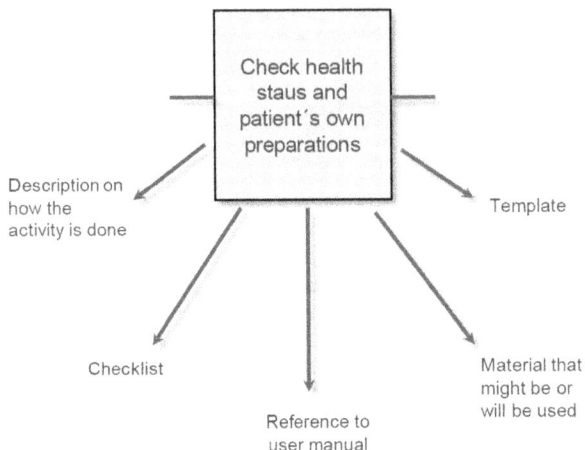

Figure 5.7 Example of how different documents may be connected to a single activity

Project Plan Example

Whether the management system is designed for small or big organizations, the project should fall to where most value for the customer of the operations is delivered. If you run a healthcare business, start working on processes and procedures connected to the patient care and near-patient activities. One way to plan the project is by following an activity plan, aiming to establish a structure that will help you to divide the project into smaller parts and to connect it to a schedule. The purpose and ultimate objective for each activity included in the project should be known and clear for all members and participants of the project group. In order to create clarity, prepare as follows:

- Decide how the activities will be performed, for example, the seminars or workshops.
- Estimate whether initial risk analysis is needed, that is, activity has impact on the project progress.
- Find out if the required prerequisites are in place.
- Is the planned schedule realistic?
- Check if the seminars and workshops are planned with dates, the rooms are booked, and the participants are invited.

- Which decisions are to be made and who is needed to participate?
- Who is responsible for each respective part of the project activity?
- How is the follow-up to be done?
- Who is to be informed and how?

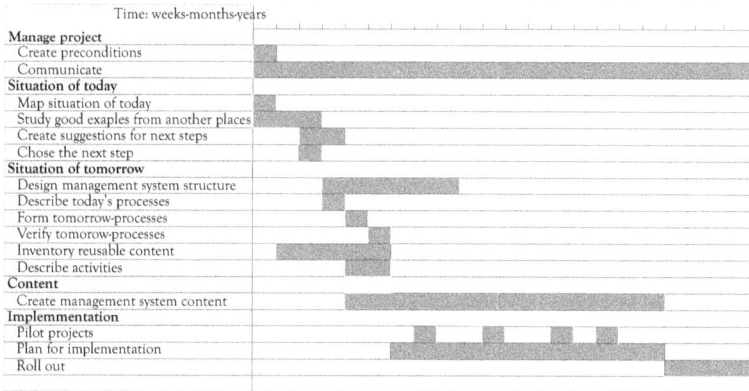

Time: weeks-months-years
Manage project
Create preconditions
Communicate
Situation of today
Map situation of today
Study good exaples from another places
Create suggestions for next steps
Chose the next step
Situation of tomorrow
Design management system structure
Describe today's processes
Form tomorrow-processes
Verify tomorow-processes
Inventory reusable content
Describe activities
Content
Create management system content
Implementation
Pilot projects
Plan for implementation
Roll out

Figure 5.8 Example of a project plan running a management system project

The Figure 5.8 depicts an example of a project execution plan. The purpose of the figure is to give you a suggestion of the sequence of activities and a suggestion about how much time to assign. The illustration does not explain if the project is planned to take three weeks or three years; it shows the proportions between activities.

The main rule is rather to plan for many minor projects with small scope, rather than a few vast ones. Small step projects succeed far more often because they are less complex and less risky. Moreover, results from small subprojects can be rolled out faster, providing the project group with important insights early in the process, and create value to the organization faster. Vast projects are often focused on fast results and due to lack of success are often put down without delivering value and desired effects.

CHAPTER 6

Implement the Management System for Patient-Safe Care

There is nothing more difficult to take in hand, more perilous to conduct, or more uncertain in its success, than to take the lead in the introduction of a new order of things.
—N. Machiavelli in "The prince," Italy, 1469–1527

Implementing a management system means putting a plan into progress and then accomplishing it by specifically creating a practical effect, and finally ensuring actual fulfillment using concrete measures. It is quite usual for a management system project in a bigger organization to go on for two to five years before being fully implemented. During this time the management system is designed, filled with content, and rolled out in subprojects. The goal is to make the management system a vivid part of organizational operations. A lot of information activities, education, support, patience, engagement, and endurance are also required.

Implementation and Implementation Activities

The implementation science (Grimshaw et al, 2004) suggests the following strategies to be generally effective:

1. Educational outreach visits
2. Interactive education sessions-based principles of adult learning
3. Targeted multifaceted interventions including two or more of the following:
   a. Audit and feedback
   b. Reminders
   c. Local consensus process
   d. Marketing

This means that it is not enough to inform the new management system about a meeting or to send an e-mail and put up some posters, believing implementation has been done and then expect people to follow it. As with everything else, implementation requires knowledge, planning, time, and commitment.

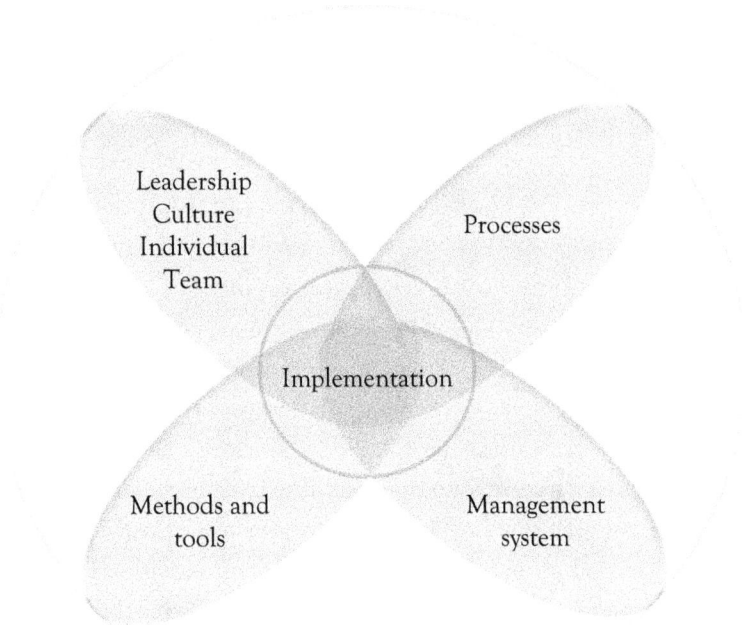

Figure 6.1 The complexity of implementation

The implementation is a complex process in itself and therefore deserves thorough preparation. It is about making change, not just in the technical environment but most of all on the personal and behavioral level. Therefore, all aspects of implementation should be seriously considered and taken into account throughout the whole implementation process. If you ignore one of the aspects shown in Figure 6.1 then you should expect more resistance to change, and a longer time for people to adapt to the new management system. Before the management system is rolled out, it is a good idea to plan for the following activities:

- Create a "good enough" release-edition of the management system, not one necessarily perfect in all details, but one good enough to start gaining detectable benefits by using the new management system.
- "Freeze" or in another way version-mark the content, making it clear for people who contribute to filling in the management system with content about what parts have been released.
- Move the management system version from projects work environment to the operating environment and make it available to the whole organization.
- Produce required material, for example, handbooks, flyers, brochures, and management system binders if needed. Many management systems are supported by IT, but there are places where binder systems are used as well.
- Roll the management system out. Electronics-supported management system is rolled out by opening portals, distributing news pages, and promoting them on the intranet. The binder-based management system is to be distributed by available logistic solutions.
- Shut down replaced parts of the current management system.
- Clean up the content in binders, the intranet content, the files on shared storage and other storage places.

Rolling out management systems is like rolling out a new IT system. Change management is more about changing behaviors than handling the system. As mentioned earlier, I recommend implementing the management system piece by piece. It is much more successful than "the big bang-way." The new part of the management system must replace the corresponding old part, and function during the transition period, alongside the current and still functioning management system. As with an IT system, using the replaced parts and versions of the management system should be prevented. Otherwise many people will continue using the old parts.

You might wonder where to start. Begin at one place and go on from there. Continue developing the system and let it mature. Perhaps eventually you will integrate it with other management systems in the organization. Start implementing where the benefits will have the most impact and where there is both need and demand. It is crucial to show good examples of usefulness and effects in a short time. When the personnel are supported and helped in their daily work, then the news about the benefits of the management system will spread throughout the organization. It will help to create engagement and a feeling of ownership of the content. The facilitators must be able to function in a flexible and responsive way to tailor their approach to the particular issues, settings, and people involved during the implementation process. Internal and external facilitators should therefore have the right level of knowledge and skills in supporting and mentoring.

As there will be an upcoming need of education and information about the management system, making a communication plan is a good idea. The communication plan should define which information is to be given, how, when, why, and to whom. The information should be customized to the receiver, delivered multiple times and in different ways, for example, text, video, or demonstration. The education should engage all personnel and executives at all levels. Create meeting platforms, enabling discussions and improvement suggestions. Keep the communication plan updated and don't hesitate to adjust it when needed. During the rolling out process it is quite usual to discover new stakeholders who need information and education. It is just not possible to foresee everything in advance, so I recommend you to arm yourself with patience and a forgiving attitude, instead of expecting perfection in every detail from the first day. Perfection may turn to become the enemy of the good. As work proceeds you will have the chance to refine the information in all the channels that you are using.

Create Engagement

Everything happens through conversations!

—Judith E. Glaser

Ability and the need to communicate are hardwired into every human being helping us to navigate successfully with others, through body language, spoken language, and conversations. Our brain has the ability to send us signals and inform us about whether the connection feels trustful or distrustful. This information creates a state of mind which directly impacts what kind of conversations we have and how we interpret them. In other words, our conversations have an impact on the level of how much we trust someone; Judith Glaser calls that *Conversational Intelligence®* (Glaser E. Judith, 2014). In the same way, success or failure when creating content for the management system and making it into an integrated platform for knowledge and best practice share point depends on how the connection, engagement, and communication are stimulated during the cocreation and engagement process. In order to create real engagement, humans need to feel trust toward the organization and feel trusted by executives and colleagues.

The level of trust depends on communication skills at all levels, which determines an organization's culture and level of psychological safety. It is important that there is quality-culture based upon values that support delivering quality-outcomes and a quality-mindset. Expectations on the management system will guide the development further; therefore it is necessary that executives provide time for reflection, learning, and information. Managers shouldn't rush and be prepared for resistance to change. They will have to use their best change management skills during the implementation phase. Top executives have a crucial role in the success, showing their engagement by being visible, by listening, by talking, by giving and receiving information, and of course by being a role model using the management system. All executives at all level shall *walk the same talk* to win credibility to the change process the organization is going through. Some ideas on creating engagement are presented here:

- Engage personnel at the sharp end early in the process, for example, by making the management system a permanent point on the agenda at weekly meetings.
- Create concise information material that is useful when informing a new employee and other parties who benefit from the knowledge.
- Prepare activities like quiz and reword engagement by making short filmed interviews to be shown on the intranet.
- Never shame or blame anyone, but always encourage, inspire, and give support.
- Use already well worked-in local knowledge and know-how which are necessary to make the workflow run every day. This way you create a feeling of connection, ownership, and cocreation of the content.
- Do not underestimate people's common sense, knowledge, and potential.
- Create a space for taking initiatives and self-determination.
- Share the benefits and find engaged personnel to become internal ambassadors for quality and superusers of the management system.
- Involve executives.
- Anchor the work to involved units and the organization as a whole.
- Celebrate shared success.

Assign Content Ownership

Many management systems "suffer lost in actuality." It is like an illness, the information is rarely updated and therefore often not to be relied on, which makes the information quality poor. The personnel quickly learn not to trust the content, because the content ownership is indistinct, or the reliability is not directed on the right path. To avoid this, all material and all knowledge stored in the management system should be managed and honored by roles holding the following responsibilities:

- *Ownership responsibility for the management system* means to have the utmost responsibility for a part of the management system within a specialty or general procedure applicable throughout the organization. It is a role for an assigner, high up in a hierarchy, and may coincide with being accountable for the actual part of the operations.

- *Maintenance responsibility for management system content* implies making sure the management system content is correct. It means that when the management system is followed and used as support, it contributes to achieving operational and organizational objectives, which, as I see it, is the main point of having a management system. Maintaining the management system means an author's role performed by people working at the sharp end, who know the work *as done*, and work on the management system content on behalf of the assigner.

- *Structure responsibility for the management system content* means to be responsible for the content quality concerning wording, comprehensiveness, compliance to the management system principles, honoring the structure, and guarding the user friendliness. It is an editing role and should be done in a process of cocreation, together with the performer of the maintenance role. The role implies also having knowledge of the responsibility structure, making sure the changes in the management system are done by people with a mandate to do so.

The rule of thumb is not to insert anything into the management system unless the responsibility structure has been followed. Over time it helps having the content in control and keeping the system up to date and reliable. Otherwise a risk arises that people with professional authority and power will make changes to the content whenever it is convenient for them, without being concerned about structuring responsibly. I'm not saying this is a job for a few chosen people. People who work in maintaining the management system have the responsibility but may very well engage others in doing the work.

To build up this kind of responsibility in your organization by appointing those responsibilities, you will need approval from the highest executive, simply because then the responsibility for the management system will become a part of the general responsibility for the entire organization. If there is already a process organization, it may be used for the responsibility structure of the management system. Usually in a process-oriented organization there is already a process owner who formally owns the process at a high level. There is also a process leader making sure that processes have been properly designed. These two roles match the owner-role and the maintenance-role for the management system well.

Identify IT Tool Requirements

The management system can be stored in different ways. Usually some of the following storage places are used for launched management systems:

- Printed documents stored in the binders and original documents stored at the administrator office (old school)
- Documents stored in a folder structure on a shared storage disc or the intranet (risky)
- Share-point or other sharing folder technique with cross-references, tags, and structured admission control and version handling (possible enough for many)
- Relational database including repository with portals and searching functions (such as Qualiware or QPR[1]) that can dynamically connect processes, documents, roles, places, legal demands, and so on (luxury)
- Support for workflows in the support information system, where the management system in large parts is implicitly built into the system (good, but hard to change)

The basics for formulating demand on the IT system are simple. Have the operations as a starting point and strive for as simple a solution as possible. It may be easy to be impressed by fancy IT solutions, but it is

---

[1]   https://qualiware.com and https://qpr.com

also easy to buy a solution that doesn't meet operational and organizational demands on support. If you are running your first management system project don't start by buying an advanced system, since you don't yet know what kind of system you need.

Start by using a simple solution and build up "ownership and responsibility organization" (previous chapter) for the management system content. When you have started to use the management system, and the management for the management system is working well, you will then have a good basis of requirements and can take the requirement specification process to the next level. When you are ready for a more competent IT support system for the management system, it should be looked at in the same way as you would look at any other IT system, that is, the IT system should offer support according to the needs and give the operational effect you strive for. As always there are general demands on IT tools, such as requirements on the technical environment, security and access control, robustness, accessibility, and costs. Moreover, there are some specific requirements for management system support:

- *Contents requirement.* Text, figures, drawings, charts, sound, video, and so on. Tagging and linking. Glossary. Description fields: operations, specialty, process, activity, role, stake holder, post, organizational structure, material, geographic structure, requirements together with how all these are related
- *User requirement.* User groups. Structures or points of entry for different kinds of users. Access control for user groups. Search engines. Usage logs
- *Maintenance.* Managing content structures. Managing accountability and responsibility. Support for content reusage. Version handling

CHAPTER 7

Live With the Management System for Patient-Safe Care

Every system is perfectly designed to give the result it gives.
—Dr. Edward Deming

When a patient is harmed while receiving health care, traditional patient safety management is mainly focused on searching for adverse events, finding failures, investigating reasons, and sucking guilty ones. It should, however, be a reason for having a deeper look at how the system is designed, how the work is organized, what support the personnel at the sharp end is given, and what kind of leadership is mirrored in the current corporate culture.

The question arises whether the management system can contribute to increased patient safety or not. In my opinion, if it can at nuclear plants, then it can in health care too.

The main forces that make a management system vivid and dynamic are based upon the quality of its structure, its ability to be maintained, and cocreating the content, building a learning organization, strongly connected to the corporate culture. In the previous chapter we looked at the principles for design, maintenance, and responsibility. In the best of worlds, a solid and durable structure is created, the content is good, and so is the technical platform on which the system is stored and operated. However, people tend to do as they like. Why? Usually this is due to inconsistent and dominant leadership, which in turn creates a culture that has a lack of trust and poor psychological safety.

Learning Organization

In the absence of learning, organizations, and individuals working in house, old practices will simply be repeated. A learning organization is an organization skilled at creating, acquiring, and transferring knowledge, and at modifying its behavior to reflect new knowledge and insights[1]. Therefore, a learning organization may be recognized by the ongoing process of learning by doing and sharing know-how knowledge. Everybody, at all levels, learns and shares. The personnel systematically learn from each other and share their experiences contributing to continuous improvements. Gained knowledge is not seen as private property but is shared generously, aiming to extend collective knowledge. This process is based on an insight that continuous improvement requires an organizational and individual commitment to learning. This description coincides with the Safety-II approach teaching us that success in delivering safe performance lies in understanding why things go right. It also lies in the exceptional human capability to adjust to an ongoing workflow and choose the best way to get things done, with respect to the current context.

In this context, the management system cannot be rigid and demand absolute compliance and obedience, driven by fear, blame game, or false rewards. In order to deliver safer care and health care, the frontline personnel must be given time for daily reflection on what went right, how, and why. Creating a space for understanding why procedures work enhances understanding when procedures move into the gray zone where risks may occur (Wears, Hollnagel and Braithwaite 2015).

When the main focus in working on safety lies on finding faults and the flawed, a culture of fear and shame builds up quickly. Fear of being named as the bad apple stimulates very strong defensive mechanisms in humans, in order to protect them from feeling shame and guilt (Dekker 2012). Amalberti et al.[2] points out a number of constraints to an ultra-safe healthcare system where three of them are related to health care's culture of individualism. The culture within healthcare systems still suffers from the individualistic view of competence, meaning that incompetence is also the fault of an individual. Health care very often takes the view that patient harm can be blamed on individual incompetence and can

---

[1] https://hbr.org/1993/07/building-a-learning-organization
[2] Amalberti, R., Y. Auroy, D. Berwick, and P. Barach. 2005. "Five System Barriers to Achieving Ultrasafe Health Care." *Annals of Internal Medicine* 142, no. 9, pp. 756–764.

be corrected by taking that "bad apple" out of the system, ignoring local rationality, degraded systems, and unsafe working environments. That can be changed by promoting learning organization where the main focus lies instead on role models and common cocreated best practices. The safety climate may then change slowly toward trust, where good leadership and safety saturates the organization. Responsible executives throughout the whole management hierarchy must establish a prestigeless environment of trust in order to achieve a climate for continuous improvement and learning.

In the management system context, the good circle, depicted in Figure 7.1 shows the way to get everyone together to build collective knowledge and to share it for the benefit of the whole organization and its customers. It is impossible to describe everything and it shouldn't be described either. If the personnel are aware of the evidence and the benefits, and if the implementation process is practical, it is more likely to be adopted (Carthey et al. 2011). Frontline staff should easily be able to find required and important information when needed. Information ought to be placed following an agreed logic, durable structure and consequently complying with agreed principles. When sharing experiences to do with successful

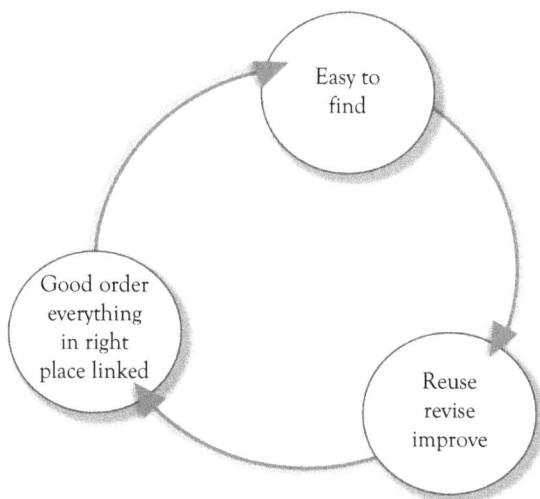

Figure 7.1 The good circle

operations and work methods, knowledge will be brought in from the broad field where most of the activities are carried out successfully, and in this way the number of adverse events will gradually be reduced.

Figure 7.2 What makes an organization a learning organization

Learning organizations are not built overnight. The success comes from carefully cultivating attitudes, commitments, and clear strategies conducted by managers who work on creating learning organization and psychological safety, slowly and steadily over time. Figure 7.2 summarizes the benefits from being an learning organization and what is needed to become one.

David A. Garvin,[3] professor at Harvard Business School, recommends taking some simple steps in order to start the process. The first step is to create an environment that promotes learning. Again, the managers must give time and space for reflection, learning, and analysis. It is difficult to learn feeling stressed and pressure. Consequently, the top management must free up employees' time. At St. Görans Hospital in Stockholm, Sweden, the waiting time for a doctor at the EU was dramatically reduced when the most experienced doctors began to work

---

[3] https://hbr.org/1993/07/building-a-learning-organization

on the front line. They did so because senior doctors noticed that the younger and less experienced colleagues learned faster and gained more knowledge when doing so. Reduced time waste and increased patient satisfaction were the side effects and not the main driving force. In other words, this created an unexpected reward and improvement. Opening up psychological and organizational boundaries and stimulating a broad exchange of ideas increases a flow of information and creates a feeling of working together instead of giving a feeling of isolation. It can be done by creating internal conferences and multi professional meetings and encouraging to eat lunch with someone unknown or staffing project teams with people from across the organization. Learning from the patients, their family members, suppliers, or internal groups and sharing ideas is another step toward creating collective knowledge and a culture of "we" and inclusiveness.

Take surgical care as an example. Individual surgeons no longer deliver surgery. Nowadays, surgery is performed and delivered by multiprofessional teams within complex systems. One surgeon's individual competence is insufficient for the optimal completion of a surgical operation. To achieve the highest levels of performance and patient safety, the whole operating theater team needs to have a shared body of knowledge about both the procedure and the system, from brain surgeon to the cleaning staff. The concept of competence as an individual possession deflects people's attention from systems thinking in health care.

One of management's big challenges and tasks is to eliminate barriers that impede learning. The other is to promote learning on the organizational agenda through the whole organization. Moreover, Garvin suggests a slight shift in focus away from continuous improvement and toward a commitment to learn. By encouraging reflection, by building teams who learn, creating psychological safety, by coaching personnel to overcome defensive interpersonal dynamics that inhibit the sharing of knowledge and ideas, leaders can make organizational learning truly happen.[4]

---

[4] Edmondson, A.C. 2012. *Teaming: How Organizations Learn, Innovate, and Compete in the Knowledge Economy*. Jossey-Bass.

Culture and Safety

Culture eats strategy for breakfast.

—Peter Drucker

The phrase, coined by the "man who invented the management," is as true as ever. If the culture is unclear, sprawling, and strongly affected by professional ego and subcultures, underestimated by management, the strategies and management systems are about to fall like dominoes.

The usefulness and benefits of the management system for patient-safe care are dependent on the corporate safety culture, management awareness about what is supported and what is tolerated, conscious leadership, and people's commitment to continuous improvements. In an interview while I was doing research for this book, a safety engineer at a Swedish nuclear plant encapsulated a management system for safety in one word—*culture*, meaning that culture is the real management system. The aim of the management system is to illustrate strategies, to describe operational objectives, and to give prerequisites to the processes in order to fulfill the objectives.

Organization, by definition, consists of people who are working in order to achieve the organization's objectives (Sveningsson, S. and Alvesson, M. 2016). People working together may share the same meaning system, values, and basic assumptions related to daily work. Or they may not. Leadership should always be looked at in the light of the context it is performed in. This means that personnel always interpret what the management does and says, as well as what the management does not do and say. These signals are crucial to how the leadership is perceived. In practice, it means that considerable attention should be devoted to understanding the connection between management's words and actions, versus employee's work and actions. Understanding the gap and insights on the impact could be a starting point for rebuilding a corporate culture toward trust and safety.

Moreover, the corporate culture mirrors the atmosphere of society which makes it just as important to reflect on your own thoughts about accountability and responsibility, your view on justice, or your awareness of how strong the forces of shame and guilt are. The disaster at the Fukushima Nuclear Plant on March 11, 2011, was described by Chairman Kiyoshi Kurokawa: "What must be admitted—very painfully—is that this was a disaster 'Made in Japan.' Its fundamental causes are to be found in the ingrained conventions of Japanese culture: our reflexive obedience; our reluctance to question authority; our devotion to 'sticking with the program'; our groupism; and our insularity."[5] There is a serious lesson for the rest of the world to learn from this insightful statement.

Culture has traditionally been symbolized as an iceberg, where above the surface the visible culture attributes are shown as objectives, goals, visions, operation plans, documents, and other descriptions. All these, above-surface attributes, describe "what we say, we are doing." As you know, the biggest part of the iceberg lies below the surface, hiding the most powerful culture attributes such as common assumptions, informal leadership, behavioral patterns, thoughts, feelings, shared stories, norms, commitments, values, and unwritten rules. The below-surface attributes together are not only talking about "how we do things around here" but are proven in action. Consequently, culture's visible attributes will either provide the culture with essential nourishment or stand out as fancy words about values written on mouse pads. There is an urgent need for management to "walk the talk" when creating a corporate culture that supports psychological safety and its extent in patient-safe health care. As long as there is a gap between "what we say, we are doing" and "how we do things around here," patients will get injured through unsafe procedures, the costs for health care will rise, and many very skilled personnel will run out of strategies to cope and quit their jobs or even take their own lives.

Conscious leaders who are present, committed, brave to have meaningful conversations that bring about desired values and objectives, cocreated by management and frontline personnel in agreement, perform leadership promoting safety. Words and actions must go hand in hand.

---

[5]   https://world-nuclear-news.org/Articles/Fukushima-a-disaster-Made-in-Japan

Leadership and Safety

When people fail to speak up with their concerns or questions, the physical safety of customers or employees is at risk, sometimes leading to tragic loss of life.

—Amy C. Edmondson (2019)

Reading so far, I hope you have a new perspective on safety management. You have learned the basics of process modeling and you understand the importance of following the principles for a management system structure when designing it. You know what is needed due to successful project outcome and what learning organization means. There is one piece left though and perhaps the most important one. I'm talking about leadership and its indisputable connection when creating patient safety. These concepts are inseparable. Leadership is like air; it is everywhere in all different aspects of an organization and drives the work forward. Directors, managers, heads, chiefs, executives, or bosses, whatever the title is, their leadership plays a crucial role when creating prerequisites for a successful management system project aiming toward improved patient safety.

The ongoing shifts in today's organizations result in high expectations in management's ability to lead in constant change and transformation. Many times, it is about changing values, shared assumptions, and behaviors. It is usually easy to lead people to where they want to be but much more challenging to lead people to where they should be (Jacobsen 2004). In order to meet the demands of the future, management needs to work using trust-based leadership. Leaders must be courageous, be visionary, and have the ability to listen and to influence and have good clinical skills. They need to dare to solve problems by trusting in their personnel's ability to find the best solutions in frontline work. It can only be done in a space of trust where transparency is founded. I mentioned "to walk the talk" earlier. It means, for example, high executives' engagement showed in being present, attending meetings, and rolling out activities and showing that working on patient safety in all aspects, for example, management system, is prioritized.

Managers should remember that frontline staff seldom have control over

- Education and training possibilities
- Work process design and complexity
- Tools and equipment
- Maintenance practices
- Products and services
- And most of all, supervisor's openness level of involvement and leadership skills

Unclear leadership gives uncertain direction on strategies and values, consequently leading to conflicting priorities (Michael Beer, 2016) and builds a culture of distrust in organization. Therefore, it is of great importance that senior executives, leaders, and managers:

- Work as a team, committing to new directions and acknowledging necessary changes in their own behavior
- Have the ability to coordinate across businesses and functions, based on robust organizational design
- Assign leadership time and devoted attention to personnel issues
- Cocreate a corporate culture where employees have no fear of telling the senior team about obstacles to the organization's effectiveness.

Data derived from a Swedish component of the cross-sectional, multinational EU seventh framework project, Registered Nurse Forecasting (RN4CAST), shows the connection between registered nurses' (RNs') assessments of patient safety and their work environment. Lisa Smeds Alenius in her PhD thesis points at some modifiable factors that have had most influence on RNs' assessments on patient safety. The factors are:

- Adequate staffing
- Adequate resources
- Management prioritizing patient safety

- Supportive nurse leadership
- Good working relations with physicians

A factor such as the size of the hospital, geographical location, or teaching status showed to have little influence on RNs' assessments of their work environment, the quality of care, or work situation. Alenius (2019) found that *"RNs subjective assessments of excellent patient safety and quality of care to be related to considerably lower odds of patients dying within 30 days of admission. This suggests RNs' assessments may be utilized as valid indicators to inform hospital managers on policy decisions regarding patient care."*

The report about safety climate in healthcare and care settings from University of Gothenburg points out the importance of allocating time for interdisciplinary reflections and the need to form working procedures collectively, to conduce a safety climate. Regulatory alignment in the Safety-I approach, and the inclusion in Safety-II approach, needs to move in parallel, as it caters for separate needs in the safety management. Writing down information in a management system is one of many ways to concretize the daily work close to the patient, which is the essence of the organization, making it visible. By managing this, managers must create a space for psychological safety.

Maintain the Management System

Accountability and responsibility for the management system should be cleared by assignment descriptions and descriptions for how to maintain the management system. The system can be vivid by protecting its well-defined structure. This task is easier to accomplish when there is a management system for the management system. There you can find the descriptions of the structure, the principles for making the content, and how to maintain the management system for patient-safe care, at the same time retaining the quality of structure and content. There are also descriptions outlining who is accountable for preserving the system's quality. At one of the Swedish nuclear plants, about 10 percent of the personnel work on management system quality, suggesting the outlook on management system's importance connected to safety and quality. Care providers should identify where cooperation with other parties happens using a more proactive approach, that is, focusing on prevention by raising awareness, sharing best practices, and understanding why things go right. Work contexts are changing all the time and many changes may cause new risks. There are several events which typically lead to updates on the management system, for example:

- New ways of how the work is done
- Improved ways of working
- Changes in procedure-related practice
- Discovered differences between management system and praxis
- Cooperation with new parts
- New technical equipment
- Change of executives
- Fusion of units
- Moving out to new facilities
- Closure of units
- New political instructions
- Reorganization

These events may be internal, external, or both. In order to uphold the quality, the personnel working on maintaining the management system have important roles and unique competencies. They should:

- Be updated knowing whether documents in management system are actual, and initiate updates when needed
- Communicate the principles to instruction and document writers and support them
- Secure information quality and readability
- Prevent gaps and overlaps in the information
- Understand the user's know-how of the management system, as well as users' shortcomings and needs
- Create a maintenance plan for keeping the system living and encourage sharp end personnel's commitment

Important questions to ask include:

- How do new employees get information about the management system for patient-safe health care?
- What kind of support is given to personnel at the sharp end by the management system for patient-safe health care?
- Are management system benefits discussed at management meetings, monthly staff meetings, and other relevant meetings?
- Is there a strategy for how to engage personnel in contributing continuously to the management system content?

The personnel working on maintaining the management may be organized by a central management system office or be placed locally in the organization and work together in an organized network.

Set Goals, Monitor, and Manage

Unless people believe that they can produce desired effects and forestall undesired ones by their actions, they have little incentive to act.
                                                —Albert Bandura (2000)

Patient safety is not only an issue for near patient workers, but very much a management concern. Consequently, the management system for patient-safe care should contain documents and procedures regarding how executives should work to promote patient-safe care and health care. Most of the healthcare organizations are based on financial funding assigned by politicians, boards, and owners. As a result, the operational objectives are set from a financial outlook and the organizations are monitored by financial and quite simple parameters. In yearly follow-ups usually the focus lies on quantitative results such as staff costs, the number of patients and hospital beds, the number of doctor consultations, how many adverse events have occurred, how many risk analyses were made, facility costs, and much more. All these are about how costs and resource are used. The annual patient safety reports are mainly focused on showing how many procedures were changed due to adverse events, but seldom describe what effects the changes led to.

In my opinion the management system for patient-safe care should contain efficacy measurements showing how patient safety is developing by:

1. Measurements that show the amount of correctly performed activities
2. Dimensions that help to understand and to improve operational processes
3. Dimensions relating to patient safety objectives that have a patient-process-focus as starting point

The efficacy measurements should be integrated in the daily work at the sharp end and be understood by people performing the work. Moreover, the measurements and monitoring for steering the operations should be derived from core operation processes. In order to be able to do so, the organization must understand the patient's complete journey through the organization when receiving health care. By doing this, new ways of working will develop and cooperation between different care providers will be improved closing dangerous gaps.

One of the many ways to achieve patient safety and good housekeeping with the resources is when the patient's pathway is as free from disturbance as possible. All personnel involved in delivering the care should be able to understand the measurements and methods used to monitor, and thereby decrease unsafe variations. Visualizing operations with process maps and explaining some parts using FRAM can give the keys to managing variations within the process (Hollnagel 2012). The personnel at the sharp end then would have the possibility of meeting and fulfilling patient's needs and expectations.

Management at all levels has an obligation to have an overview on the whole process, to be able to provide prerequisites for delivery of patient-oriented and thereby safe health care. In the short term the costs, risks, and problems can be moved into another unit but not away from the patient. A process is the place where value and customer satisfaction are created. That is why the processes should be managed, and not the functions. You need to find good methods for healthcare improvement in the ongoing daily processes if you desire effects in operation (Berwick 2008).

An excellent example of how it can be done comes from Höglands Hospital in Eksjö, Sweden. The personnel in the emergency unit noticed that an elderly person who had just received care at the hospital was quickly returned to the emergency unit again, sick and in need of care. The patient's whole process got mapped and it was discovered that many patients had had difficulties managing their medication on their own. The hospital management arranged care workshops on how to manage prescriptions and medication for selected patient groups. Moreover, communication with district nurses was improved and in a short time the number of readmissions had drastically fallen (Stigendal 2010). When the hospital management looked into the whole patient process, new questions arose, and the answers resulted in improved processes and lower costs.

The 100-year-old idea of Taylorism still steers many businesses in the correct path. Letting the administrative personnel form objectives for operations gives many examples of how wrong it can be, for example, monitoring the effectiveness of the police by counting the number of traffic checkups or by counting how many patients a doctor receives every day. Goal completion does not say much about whether more drivers drive in a sober state or if a patient's needs have been met and satisfied. Volume monitoring is important but should not be the only way of monitoring operational outcomes. It is crucial to differentiate between accomplishment and effect. Effect-focus gives a patient in the first place meaning that the choice of management philosophy mirrors what decision makers believe is important. If it is the number of appointments, then the time slots get shortened without taking quality into account, and thereby ignoring real operational objectives, for example, patient-safe health care. A quantitative measurement can be highlighted by a health center where a decided number of patient appointments are done during a definite period. When the objectives are set without understanding operational reality, just to fulfill the expected result, the following becomes apparent:

- In order to uphold the quality of the appointments, more personnel will be required. In the short term, the personnel will work extra hours and work a little faster. In the long run if no more personnel get hired, the quality in delivered care will suffer due to a lack of time. More mistakes will be made, and the costs will increase.

- Time and quality are connected. When the measurement is, for example, more appointments, the same number of personnel will have to do more work but for a longer time. The quality will be the same, but availability will decrease. The longer the patients will have to wait, the lower patient satisfaction will be, and in some cases patient safety will be affected.
- If the assigned goals affect time and staffing, and at the same time unrealistic objectives are set by, for example, boards, owners, managers, administrators, then the results will be adjusted so the degraded quality does not show up in reports and follow-ups.

The pyramid in Figure 7.3 illustrates the before-mentioned scenarios translated to patient safety and highlights how design of operational objectives affects patient safety. It also shows how important it is for management to have a knowledge of operations when setting goals and making those consistent with an organization's vision, mission, quality, patient safety, good work environment, accessibility, and finances in balance. According to Stigendal (2010), the efficient use of resources should never be the objective for operations, yet a demand on it. Cheap and fast

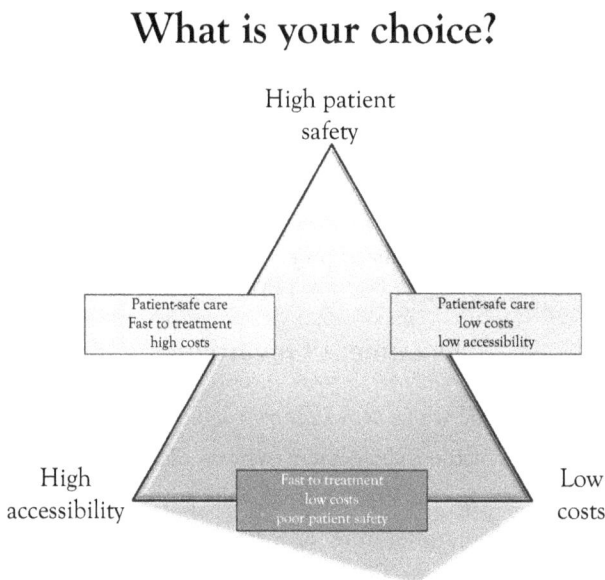

Figure 7.3 The safety pyramid

doesn't connect to high quality. Quality at low cost results in low accessibility, and patient safety will be at risk.

As an alternative or a complement to resource management philosophy there is the philosophy called *Systems thinking*. This is about seeing everything in its entirety. The main objective in the system-thinking outlook is to supply core operations with all necessary prerequisites in order to fulfill the objectives. Then the organization and the operations may formulate their own objectives, for example, more sober drivers on the roads or patients getting their prescriptions in time. An objective may also be to decrease waiting time for patients between diagnostics and treatment, or fewer acute readmissions. Multifocal glasses and hawk-eyes are needed to get there in order to see the whole picture and to discover key success factors. Management should therefore focus more on:

- Understanding how *the work at the sharp end* works
- Reusing good practices used locally, nationally, and internationally
- Making sure that changes and improvements result in desired outcomes
- Finding where improvements are needed to be done in the organization
- Reflecting on how well operations fulfill the needs of their customers, for example, the patients
- Reflecting on how well the processes are running
- Understanding which systemic factors support and which counteract the continuous process improvement

Document Governance

It is a great advantage when *document governance* and *document handling* are a natural part of the management system. *Document governance* is a management-level issue. It aims to create rules and a framework for how, where, and who may create, store, or sort out information, for example, documents stored in the management system. The document governance also creates rules for archive management. *Document handling* is a part of everybody's daily work in the organization, where personnel continually contribute to the management system by creating new documents, making information public on the intranet, sending information via e-mail, or reviewing, sorting out, or filing the information. Well-designed and consequent structure and discrimination contributes to management system quality, and so document handling is strongly related to the management system for patient-safe care. When working on implementation and management of the management system, it may be done according to the *document management plan*. In the document management plan, you can read, for example, what role determines the management system information, what role updates the information, and what role is accountable for or publishes the governing documents. This by itself is a management system for the management system.

In order to make the document governance and handling structured I recommend:

- Categorizing different document types.
- Describing who is accountable for respective document type and who is the writer of the content.
- Deciding and describing which role the final review does and defines different documents.
- Deciding the life cycle of the respective document type.
  It makes it easier to secure actuality of the information and to keep an eye on how often the documents have to be reviewed.
- Creating *Get the document known in organization*, procedures.
- Creating a plan for document management and archiving.
- Purchasing IT system to support the document management and handling, which is to be integrated to an IT-system that supports the management system.

Documents in a management system may be categorized as follows:

- Governing/describing
- Reporting/outcome document
- Technical descriptions

The governing and describing documents may need to be updated. These are the guidelines for operations, for example:

- *A policy* describes how the organization relates to certain issues like smoking, dress code, using phones and IT.
- *A guideline* gives evident support on how to act in a given context, for example, local or national guidelines for palliative care.
- *An instruction* is the unambiguously formulated way of doing things without leaving space for interpretation, for example, delivering CPR.
- *A recommendation* describes the method and utilities to be used in a given situation aimed at supporting the work as done in the best possible way, that is, best practice.

Both the reporting and the outcome documents are annual reports, financial reports, and contracts. These types of documents are usually made only in one version and the "best before date" is usually quite short. Technical descriptions are, for example, construction drawings and manuals.

A Few Words About ISO Standards

ISO stands for *International Organization for Standardization*. There are many ISO standards formed for different purposes such as for the environment, the work environment, quality, and information security. The different standards form specifications for products, services, and systems to ensure quality, efficiency, and safety, and may also be integrated to each other. Many organizations strive to follow the standards and eventually become ISO-certified. The aim is often to show the owners and customers that the quality demands are fulfilled. A management system certified by, for example, ISO-9001 may work as a basis for management and quality improvement of products, processes, and services. The certification means that the management system and the description of it:

- Fulfills the demands of the standard
- Is continually maintained
- Is reviewed in relation to the standard demands

Getting certified is a vast project and standardization is hard work to do. Together it is like working with a two-edged tool which soon may become a burden. It may become just a diploma on the wall, increased bureaucracy, and rigid regulations to be obeyed. On the other hand, it can contribute to creating a learning organization, conscious leadership, increased safety, quality, lower staff turnover, and ongoing improvements. The management system structure and content must be like a mirror of the reality, where the frontline staff can recognize themselves and feel they have ownership and control over the content. As reality changes, the management system content must reflect these changes. The success, as always, depends on how management at all levels of the organization works with the management system.

CHAPTER 8

Author's Reflections

Risks do not arise as simple and linear consequences for specific and easy-to-find reasons. Risks emerge because of ongoing variations of complex relationships and dependencies between the many activities that together constitute daily life and the variety of a workflow. Regardless of how well a management system is designed and how well it is loaded with reliable content, it is not enough to improve patient safety alone, although it helps. I have identified four major challenges when improving patient safety:

1. Poor corporate culture
2. Lack of a systemic approach in safety management
3. Main focus on things that went wrong
4. Unhealthy leadership leading to poor psychological safety

To be able to get to the real problems with insufficient patient safety, there is a great need to gather and work on the culture of the different management levels and especially on the staff level. Culture in the health care is impregnated with ambivalence where willingness to do well and to think of the patients' best in the first place is discouraged by a silo kind of thinking, knowledge field boundaries, personal and professional prestige, culture of silence, difficulties talking about difficult matters, bullying, blaming, fear of shame, and stress caused by a guilty conscience. These kind of mixed corporate cultures have grown in many workplaces for decades.

In 1982, a fatal dialysis accident occurred in Sweden. Two patients died and several more needed intensive care. Just one single nurse was held accountable despite public protests. This incident and its judicial aftermath horrified generations of nurses and physicians, both newly graduated and experienced ones. I remember receiving advice from my older colleagues: "just write everything down in the journal and stay safe." Both the media and the court verdict treated healthcare personnel like battue, and this contributed in creating a strong fear of making mistakes and of holding the entire responsibility alone. The nurse was refused a retrial, in spite of several investigations that uncovered imprecisions in the juridical process and of proven serious systemic failures (Åsard 2013).

In 2008, a single physician was pointed out as guilty for the death of an infant at the Astrid Lindgren Pediatric Hospital in Stockholm. It became known as the "Astrid Lindgren case" and was very closely watched by the media. Once more the message was clear: "if you make a mistake you have to bear the whole responsibility and guilt." There was a tremendous lack of proportion between the many miles of text in the media during the investigation and the trial compared to when the physician was actually found not guilty by the court.

These and many other similar incidents are just two examples of how strong the shame and blame culture is in western culture. Unfortunately, it is also maintained by media's one-sided search for the guilty ones (Dekker 2013). Patient safety does not demand single people guilt. It demands systemic improvements where all the cooperative actors encourage patient-safe health care and care of the elderly. It demands cocreation of patient-orientated processes, crossing organizational boundaries. The desirable systemic approach is still missing today in most workplaces and the personnel reflects a deep fear of making mistakes, of being singled out and shut out from other colleagues, career opportunities, or even losing their job. This kind of culture is based on the fear of being singled out as incompetent in a nonforgiving climate (Dekker 2012).

Unfortunately, the advice from the 1980s such as "just write everything down and stay safe" is given just as often today, as then. Generally, in health care, there is lack of readiness and a lack of procedures concerned with how to take care of the staff involved in incidents. In consequence, some individuals get hurt very badly. They stay on sick leave for a long time or even commit suicide. Healthcare personnel are supposed to work in a process-oriented way. To succeed in that, in reality, there is a need for new approaches on how the work and the collaborations are planned and executed. This challenges current management structures and the state of power.

A process ownership structure enables understanding the patient's entire journey throughout the healthcare organization. Based on that understanding it is possible to design processes, flows, supporting structures, and so on, crossing the organizational and financial boundaries. Roles investigating adverse events still have fault-focus on the patient safety. That is due to a long tradition of retrospectively writing down adverse events, of measuring faults and reporting actions against deficits. In my opinion the main focus should be on reporting successful effects that the actions led to—how many of the work procedures have been improved and how many patients got correct help. The key to success lies in understanding why an action succeeded, not why it failed. All these factors, combining a change in behavior and culture, make a difference in patient safety.

Patient safety culture is reflected in the attitudes of leaders and staff and their approach to patient safety and manifests a culture in health care. Unfortunately, the collegiality in many professions is many times very strong and for the purpose of protection many reports are never written. This kind of behavior may be caused by fear of loss of prestige, alienation, or consequences effecting career or salary. I interpret it as a clear indication that the systemic thinking has not yet been rooted either in the daily work at the sharp end or by management at all levels. Continuing is a sign of insufficient leadership and a lack of consistent leadership strategy. The cultural iceberg I have been talking about can destroy any good initiative, if its hidden power is underestimated and overlooked by management.

The culture is reflected both in the prerequisites created by politicians and owners and in the leadership, carried out by executives throughout the entire power pyramid. Then again, leadership is a change-process mediator between workers and executives, meaning the personnel also have a great share of responsibility in this context. Health care belongs to the risky workplaces. There are calculated risks which are important for the personnel to be aware of. Patients have the right to get the information about calculated risks due to procedures, treatments, and, for example, surgical interventions, in order to help patients take a stand on the treatment. But a patient should not need to calculate the risks of getting injured for a lifetime, or of dying, because the hygiene regulations were not followed or because the checklist for safe surgery were neglected or because the staff were not provided with up-to-date instructions for newly purchased medical equipment. Neither should patients have to calculate the avoidable complications due to insufficient medical records that the provided caregiver hasn't been given concerning the lifesaving information about medication prescribed at another clinic or health center. On the other hand, no one should get a pat on the back from the boss and hear "you are so good, you can do it" when putting the patient and personnel at risk.

So, how can we create a world that encourages patient safety? In my opinion safety occurs next to the patient. Safety happens at a moment where vital decisions need to be made. Thanks to human adaptability, flexibility, together with knowledge, intuition, and creativity, most of the actions succeed, where harm might have occurred. It is when reflecting over how the work is done, and by understanding the subtle nuances of variations in the daily work, a real safety climate emerges. In a true learning organization where the team members, without prestige or fear, can share their experiences and knowledge, that is where the magic of cocreation happens. Affinity arises along with a climate filled with trust and empathy, where both people and their collective knowledge grow for the best of the patient or the care recipient.

Public opinion polls suggest that most Americans have trust in their medical team. When people go to the physician or are admitted to the hospital, few of them worry about being harmed by the doctor, or someone else from the medical team making a mistake. Unfortunately, mistakes do happen and a lot of the adverse events are both preventable and serious.

The most common types of preventable harm include hospital-acquired infections, surgical errors, wrong-site surgery, medication errors, in-hospital injury, misdiagnosis, or deep vein thrombosis. Depending on the set of prevalence data used, preventable harm results in between 250,000 and 400,000 deaths annually in hospitals in the United States, which would make preventable patient harm the third leading cause of death.[1] A far more common outcome than death is serious harm, which

---

[1]   Frankel, A., C. Haraden, F. Federico, and J. Lenoci-Edwards. 2017. *A Framework for Safe, Reliable, and Effective Care*. White Paper. Cambridge, MA: Institute for Healthcare Improvement and Safe and Reliable Healthcare.

affects more than 10 to 20 times more patients than lethal harm. Preventable harm costs billions of dollars every year and inflicts a huge amount of suffering for both patients and personnel involved.

Administrators should not be the primary determinant in frontline staff's ability to deliver safe, effective, and humane care. Many countries struggle with top-heavy systems, in which decisions about how care should be provided are made by those who work at the blunt end of operational reality far away from the experience of caring for patients. This must change. Professionals at the sharp must get involved and engaged. They need support, structure, and help organizing necessary information and they need management committed to cocreation of a safe culture, learning organization, and safe patient care, at lower costs. One choice is to consider the management system as a collection of documents and a nice diploma on the office wall, fulfilling the law and owner demands. The other choice is to take height for a broader approach, including new leadership methods and proactive safety work that sincerely encourages patient safety, saves lives, eases suffering, and stops wasting money.

We do not make mistakes, we make variations!

References

Alvesson, A., and S. Sveningsson. 2016. *Changing Organizational Culture.* London and New York. Routledge.

Åsard, P.E. 2013. *Dialysolyckan: ett rättshaveri i sjukvården.* Stockholm: Bokförlaget Mormor.

Bandura, A. 2000. "Cultivate Self-Efficacy for Personal and Organizational Effectiveness." *Handbook of Principles of Organization Behavior* 2, pp. 11–21.

Beer, M., M. Finnström, and D. Schrader. October 2016. "Why Leadership Training Fails—and What to Do about It." *Harvard Business Review* 94, no. 10, pp. 50–57.

Berwick, D. 2008. "The Science of Improvement." *JAMA* 299, no. 10, pp. 1182–1184.

Carthey, J., S. Walker, V. Deelchand, C. Vincent, and W.H. Griffiths. 2011. "Breaking the Rules: Understanding Non-Compliance with Policies and Guidelines." *BMJ* 343, d5283. doi: 10.1136/bmj.d5283

Chassin, M.R., and J.M. Loeb. 2013. "High-Reliability Health Care: Getting there from Here." *The Milbank Quarterly* 91, no. 3, pp. 459–490.

Dekker, S. 2012. *Just Culture Balancing Safety and Accountability.* UK: Ashgate.

Dekker, S. 2013. *Second Victim Error, Guilt, Trauma and Resilience.* CRC Press.

Dekker, S. 2018. *The Safety Anarchist. Relying on Human Expertise and Innovation, Reducing Bureaucracy and Compliance.* London and New York. Routledge.

Edmondson, A. 2019. *The Fearless Organization Creating Psychological Safety in the Workplace for Learning, Innovation, and Growth.* Harvard Business School. New Jersey. Wiley.

Frankel A, C. Haraden, F. Federico, and J. Lenoci-Edwards. 2017. "A Framework for Safe, Reliable, and Effective Care." *White Paper.* Cambridge, MA: Institute for Healthcare Improvement and Safe and Reliable Healthcare.

Grimshaw, J., R. Thomas, G. MacLennan, C.R. R.C. Fraser, C.R. Ramsay, L.E.E.A. Vale, and M.J.P. Wensing. 2004. "Effectiveness and Efficiency of Guideline Dissemination and Implementation Strategies." *Health Technology Assessment* 8, no. 6

Hiatt, J. 2006. *ADKAR a Model for Change in Business, Government and our Community.* Prosci Learning Center Publications, Colorado.

Hollnagel, E. 2012. *FRAM—The functional Resonance Analysis Method.* Farnham, UK: Ashgate.

Hollnagel, E. 2014. *Safety-I and Safety-II: The past and Future of Safety Management.* Farnham, UK: Ashgate.

Hollnagel, E., R.L. Wears. and J. Braithwaite. 2015. "From Safety-I to Safety-II: A white paper." The resilient health care net: Published simultaneously by the University of Southern Denmark, University of Florida, USA and Macquarie University, Australia.

Glaser E.J. 2014. *Conversational Intelligence How Great Leaders Build Trust and Get Extraordinary Results.* Bibliomotion, Incorporated.

Jacobsen, D.I. 2004. *Organisationsförändringar och förändringsledarskap.* Lund: Studentlitteratur.

Ljungberg, A., and E. Larsson. 2012. *Processbaserad verksamhetsutveckling: Varför-vad-hur?* Lund: Studentlitteratur.

Reason, J. 1997. *Managing the Risk of Organizational Accident.* Aldershop, United Kingdom: Ashgate.

Smeds Alenius, L. 2019. "Conditions for Care: Factors in the Nurse Work Environment Related to Safe and High Quality Care." [Doctoral Thesis] Karolinska Institutet, Stockholm).

Stigendal, L. 2010. "Effektiv Styrning." En rapport om system- och processbaserad styrning i offentlig sektor.

Sveningsson, S. and M. Alvesson. 2016. *Changing Organizational Culture, Cultural Change Work in Progress.* London and New York. Routledge.

Tregear, R. 2016. "Reimagining Management." *Putting process at the Center of Business Management.* UK: IRM.

Törner, M., M. Eklöf, P. Larsman, and A. Pousette. 2013. *Säkerhetsklimat i vård och omsorg. Bakomliggande faktorer och betydelse för personalsäkerhet och patientsäkerhet.* Slutrapport, AFA dnr. 090002. Göteborgs universitet.

Wears, R.L., E. Hollnagel, and J. Braithwaite. 2015. *Resilient Health Care, Volume 2: The Resilience of Everyday Clinical Work.* Farnham, UK: Ashgate.

Wheelan, S. 2014. *Creating Effective Teams, A Guide for Members and Leaders.* SAGE Publications.

World Health Organization, WHO. http://who.int/patientsafety/about/en/. (accessed on April 2019).

https://iso.org/management-system-standards.html (accessed on September 2019)

https://lexico.com/en/definition/process (accessed on September 2019)

https://en.wikipedia.org/wiki/Railroad_Safety_Appliance_Act (accessed on September 2019)

https://thefreedictionary.com/safety (accessed on September 2019)

About the Author

Anita Edvinsson CRNA, B.Sc, AOCNS, is an author, trainer, speaker and patient safety advisor in public and private healthcare and social care. She is founder and principal consultant of Aurata Consulting, a company that facilitates changes towards a conscious leadership, operational efficiency and improved patient safety.

Anita Edvinsson is based in Sweden, in Northern Europe. She has a profound knowledge in the challenges that modern health care and social care are facing, owing to her long career as a ward manager, site manager, department manager and team leader in public and private care. As a leader she implemented continuous operational development as a part of the daily work, improving the health care leadership, and creating beneficial changes in health care.

She has published two titles for Swedish publishing houses. The first book is a handbook on designing, establishing and using health care management systems, especially aimed at improved patient safety. It is well -used as literature in university programs. The second book is about forming a conscious leadership to form a conscious organization. Her huge practical experience, together with an immense research prior to the books, has made her a well-requested speaker, coach and consultant.

She has an earlier background as a nurse in general health care and has a B.Sc. degree in anesthetic nursing, and, is also specialized in oncological nursing. She has also gained professional ICF Coach status. Beyond this, she has a university education in leadership, change management, and healthcare information technology.

Index

OTHER TITLES IN THE HEALTHCARE MANAGEMENT COLLECTION

- *Behind the Scenes of Healthcare by* Hesston L. Johnson
- *Predictive Medicine* by Emmanuel Fombu
- *The DNA of Physician Leadership* by Myron J. Beard
- *Management Skills for Clinicians, Volume II* by Linda R. LaGanga
- *Management Skills for Clinicians, Volume I* by Linda R. LaGanga
- *Leading Adaptive Teams in Healthcare Organizations* by Kurt C. O'Brien and Christopher E. Johnson
- *The Patient Paradigm Shifts* by Judy L. Chan

Announcing the Business Expert Press Digital Library

Concise e-books business students need for classroom and research

This book can also be purchased in an e-book collection by your library as

- a one-time purchase,
- that is owned forever,
- allows for simultaneous readers,
- has no restrictions on printing, and
- can be downloaded as PDFs from within the library community.

Our digital library collections are a great solution to beat the rising cost of textbooks. E-books can be loaded into their course management systems or onto students' e-book readers.
The **Business Expert Press** digital libraries are very affordable, with no obligation to buy in future years. For more information, please visit **www.businessexpertpress.com/librarians**. To set up a trial in the United States, please email **sales@businessexpertpress.com**.

www.ingramcontent.com/pod-product-compliance
Lightning Source LLC
Chambersburg PA
CBHW061325220326
41599CB00026B/5038